Dave Matthews
ANTHOLOGY

CONTENTS

Photography by Danny Clinch

Transcribed by Jeff Jacobson and Paul Pappas

Cherry Lane Music Company
Director of Publications/Project Editor: Mark Phillips
Manager of Publications: Gabrielle Fastman

ISBN-13: 978-1-60378-011-7
ISBN-10: 1-60378-011-4

Visit our website at www.cherrylane.com

G000150770

AMERICAN BABY

Words and Music by
Dave Matthews Band and Mark Batson

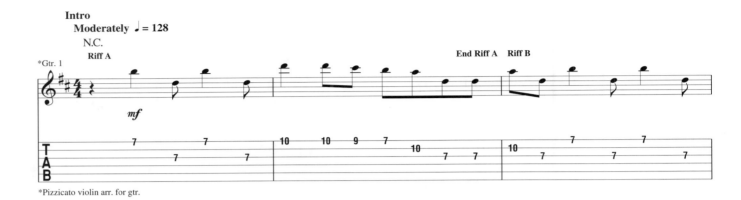

*Pizzicato violin arr. for gtr.

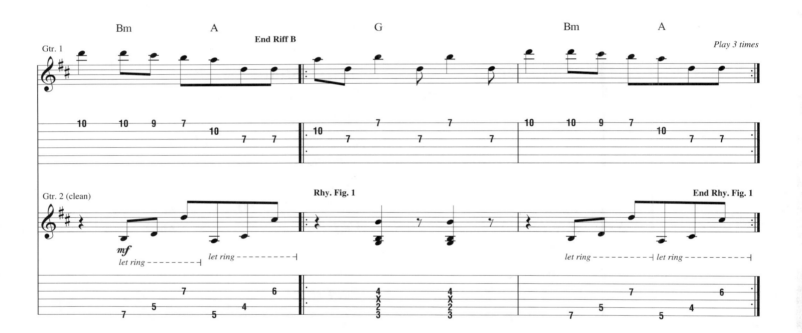

Verse
Gtr. 1: w/ Riff B (4 times)
Gtr. 2: w/ Rhy. Fig. 1 (4 times)

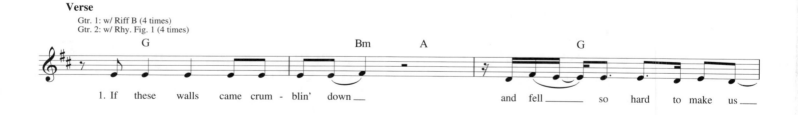

1. If these walls came crum-blin' down __ and fell __ so hard to make us __

__ lose our faith, __ from what's left you'd __ fig-ure it out __ and __

2

still make lem - on - ade taste like a sun - ny day.

Stay, ___ beau - ti - ful ba - by. I hope you

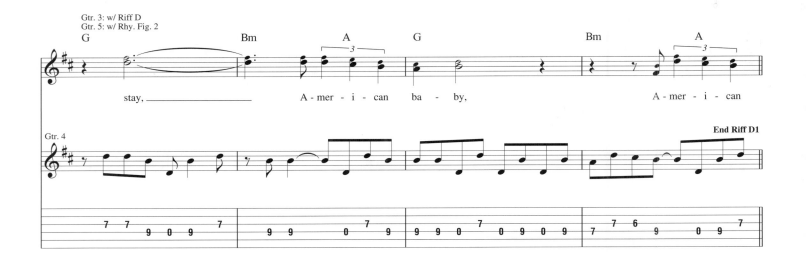

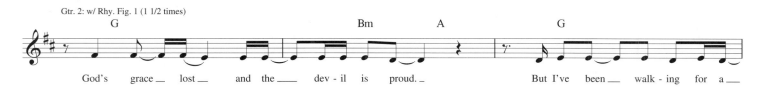

ANTS MARCHING

Words and Music by
David J. Matthews

9

THE BEST OF WHAT'S AROUND

Words and Music by
David J. Matthews

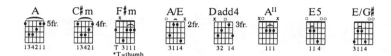

*Throughout song, all repeats (including D.S.) and all recalled rhy. figs. and rhy. fills are played with slight variations ad lib.

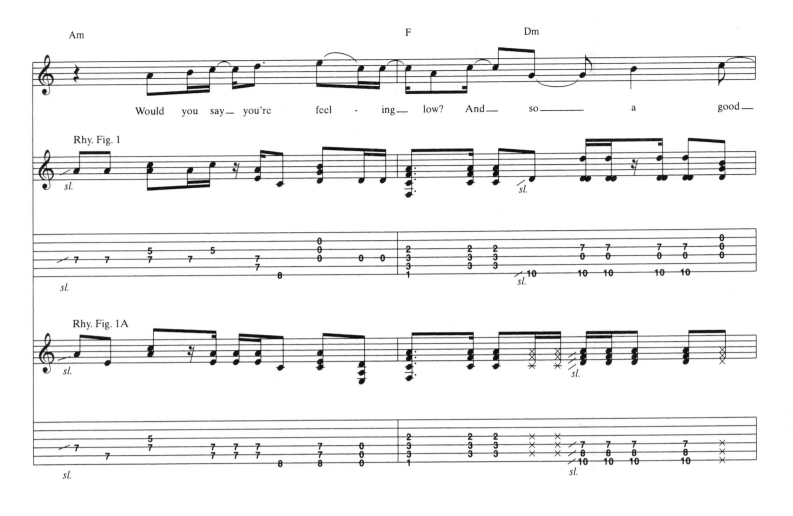

Would you say— you're feel - ing— low? And— so—— a good—

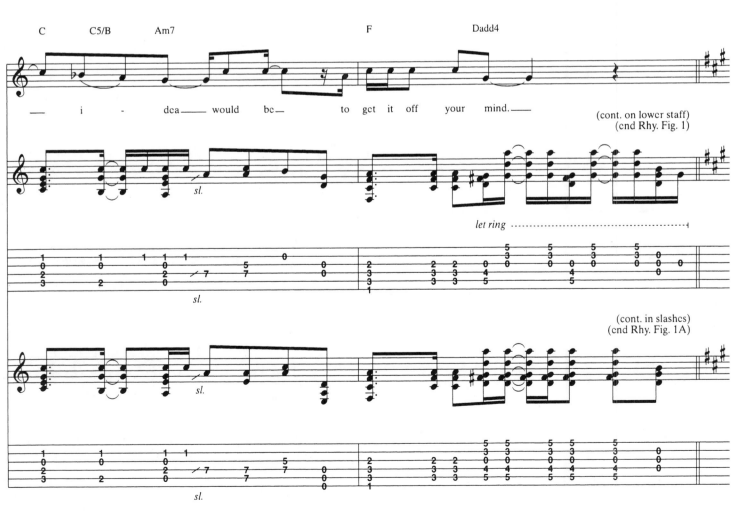

— i - dea—— would be— to get it off your mind.—

(cont. on lower staff)
(end Rhy. Fig. 1)

let ring

(cont. in slashes)
(end Rhy. Fig. 1A)

14

Additional Lyrics

2. And if you hold on tight to what you think is your thing,
   You may find you're missing all the rest.
   Well, she run up into the light surprised.
   Her arms are open. Her minds's eye is...

   2nd Chorus:
   Seeing things from a better side than most can dream.
   On a clearer road I feel, oh, you could say she's safe.
   Whatever tears at her, whatever holds her down.
   And if nothing can be done, she'll make the best of what's around. *(To Bridge)*

CRASH INTO ME

Words and Music by
David J. Matthews

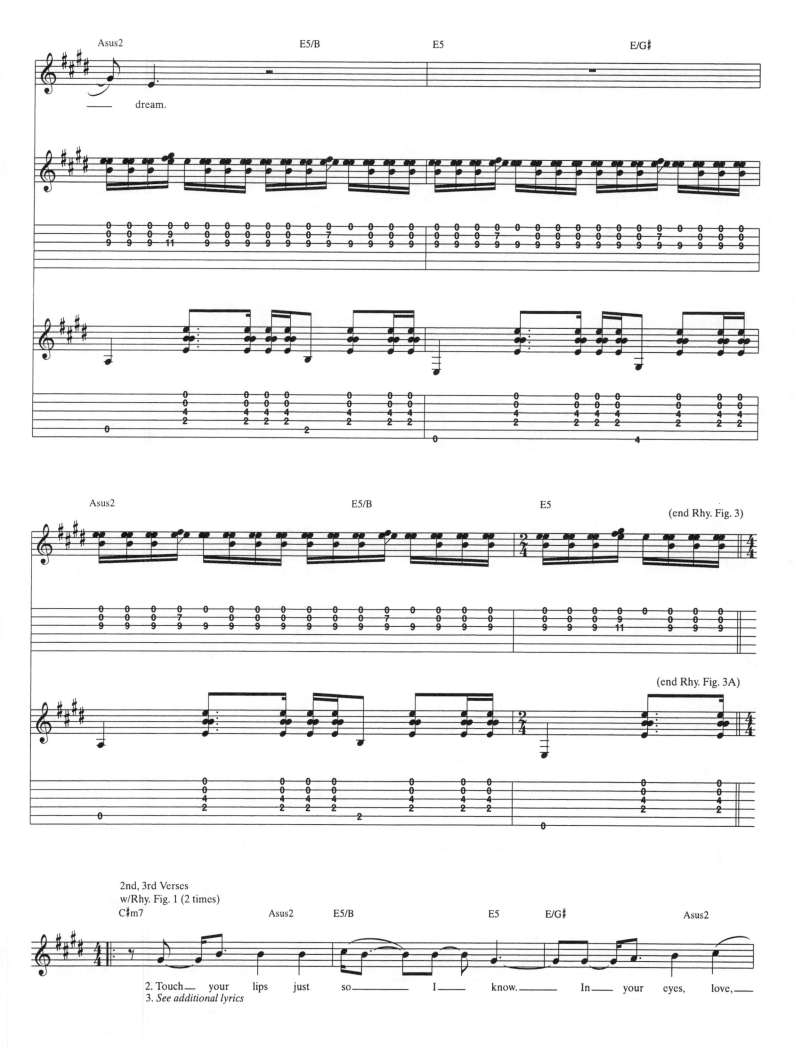

Additional Lyrics

3. Only if I've gone overboard,
   Then I'm begging you
   To forgive me, oh,
   In my haste.
   When I'm holding you so, girl,
   Close to me.
   Oh, and you come... *(To Chorus)*

CRUSH

Words and Music by
David J. Matthews

Cra - zy___ how you___ make it all al - right,___

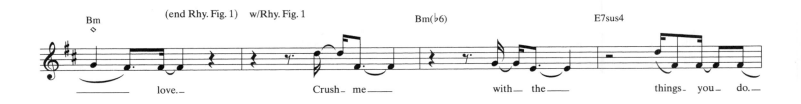

___ love.___ Crush_ me___ with_ the___ things_ you_ do.___

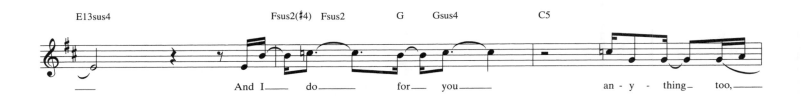

___ And I___ do___ for___ you___ an - y - thing_ too,___

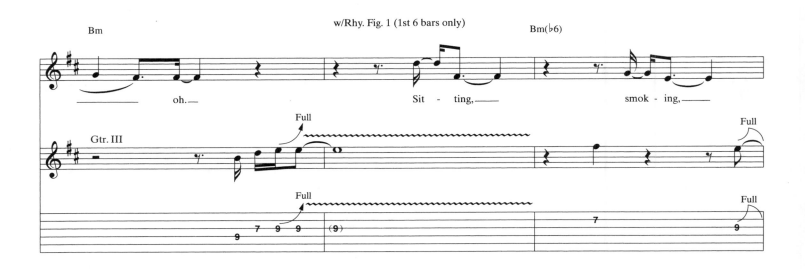

___ oh.___ Sit - ting,___ smok - ing,___

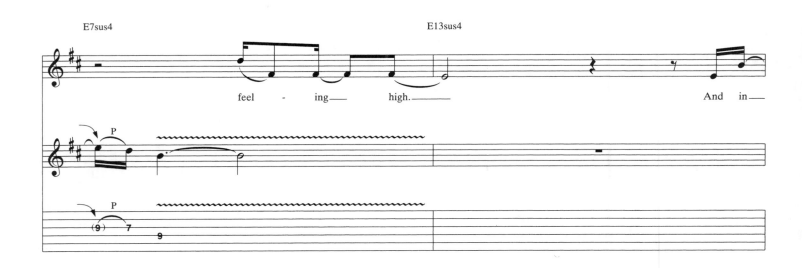

feel - ing___ high.___ And in___

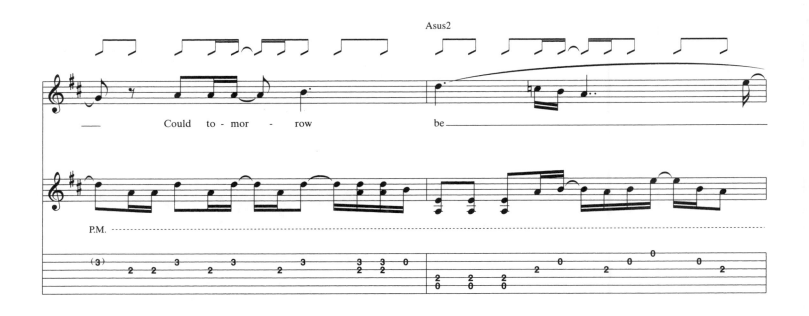

Could to-mor-row be

(end Rhy. Fig. 2)

so won-drous as you there, sleep-ing?

2nd Verse
w/Rhy. Fig. 1

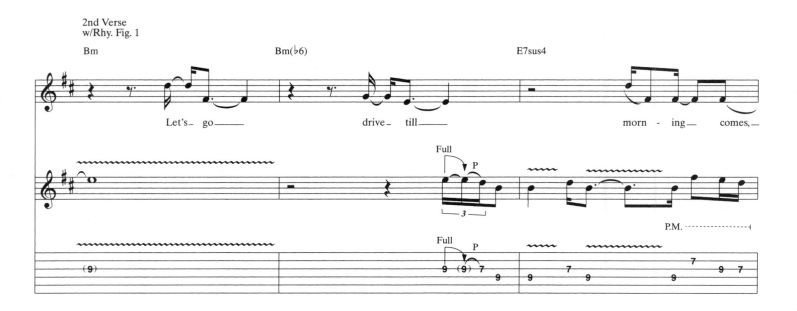

Let's go drive till morn-ing comes,

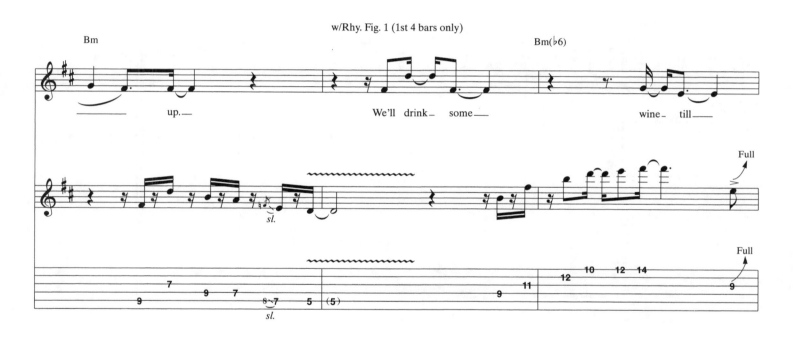

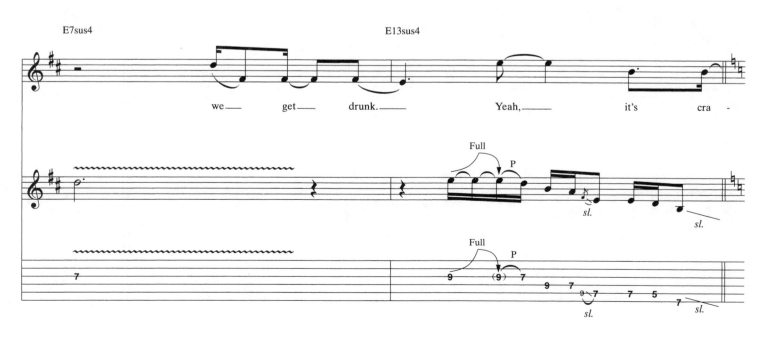

*Play w/slight variations ad lib when recalled (throughout).

Lovely lady,_____ I will treat you sweet - ly,_____
*w/slight variations ad lib

_____ a - dore you._____ I____ mean you crush_ me.____ And it's times like__ these__

____ when my faith__ I feel,_____ and_____ I____ know

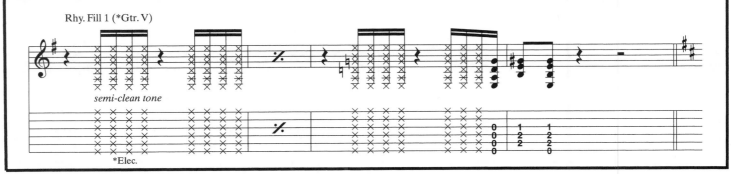

Rhy. Fill 1 (*Gtr. V)

semi-clean tone

*Elec.

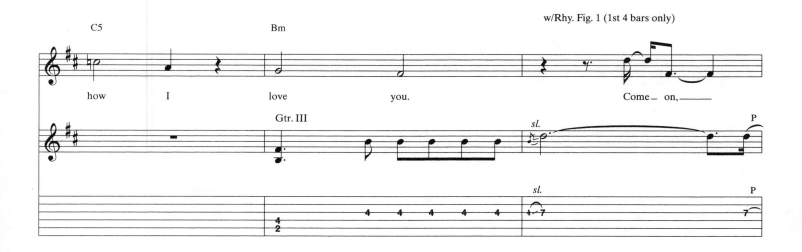

how   I   love   you.   Come on,____

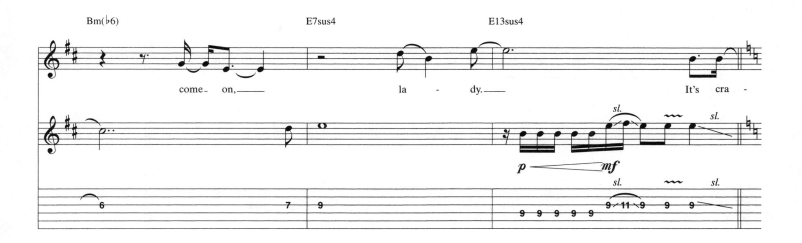

come on,____   la - dy.____   It's cra -

Chorus

w/Rhy. Figs. 3, 3A & 3B (all 1st 4 bars only)

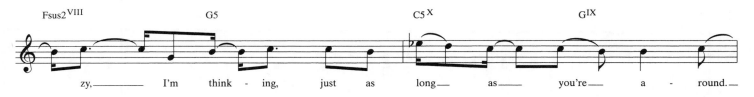

zy,____ I'm think - ing, just as long____ as____ you're____ a - round.

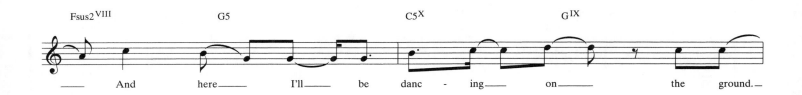

____ And here____ I'll____ be danc - ing____ on____ the ground.____

w/Rhy. Figs. 3, 3A & 3B (all bars 3 & 4 only) (all 5½ times)

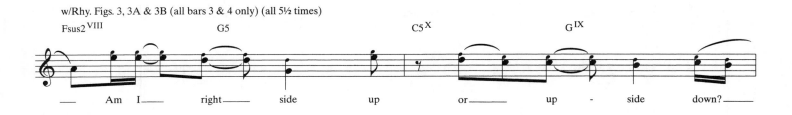

____ Am I right side up or up - side down?

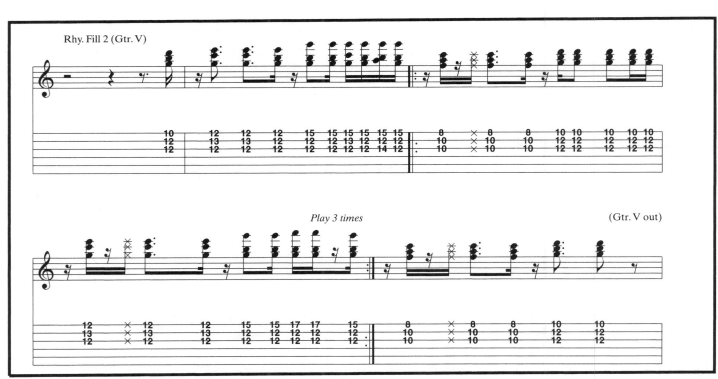

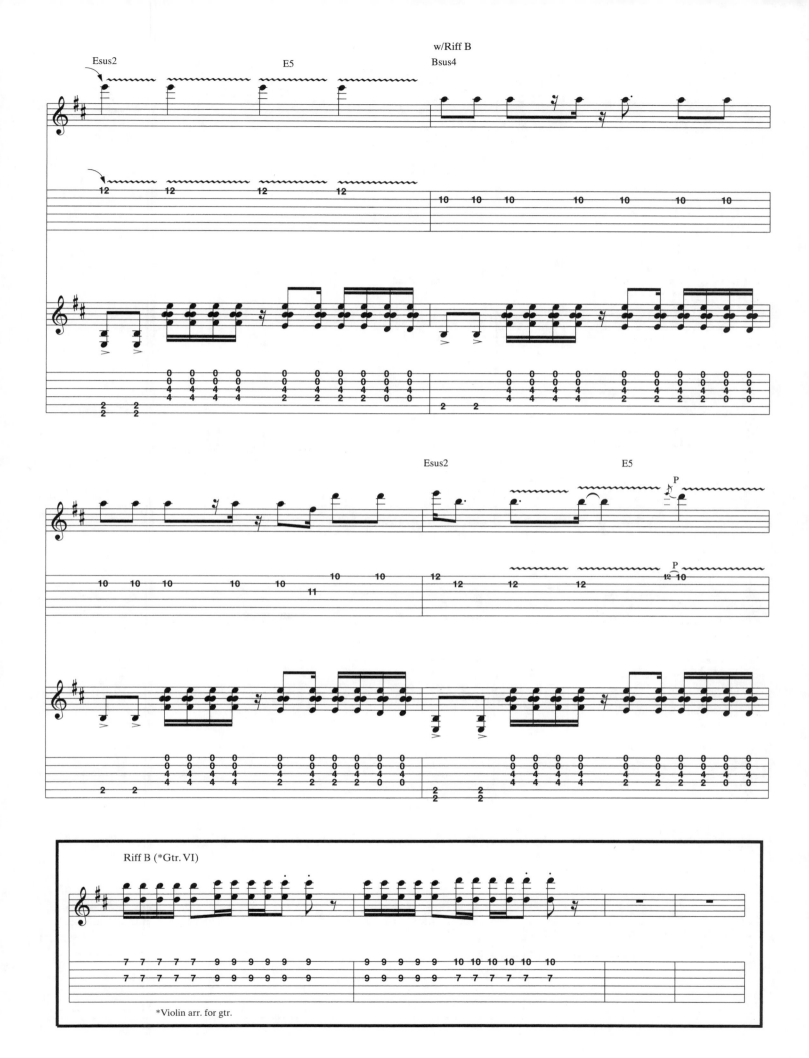

41

DANCING NANCIES

Words and Music by
David J. Matthews

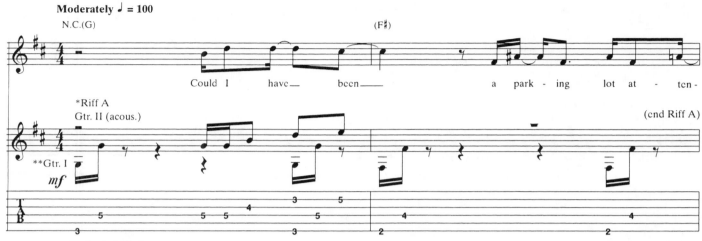

*Refers to both gtrs.
**Two acous. gtrs. arr. for one (throughout).

45

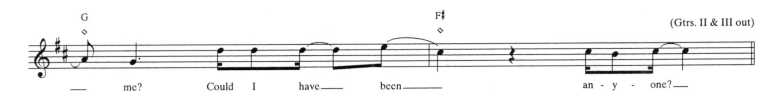

me? Could I have been an-y-one?

Faster ♩ = 116

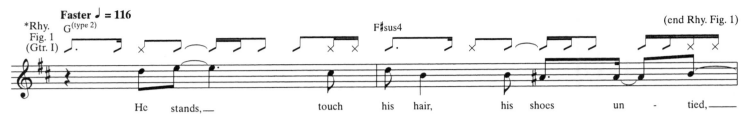

*Rhy. Fig. 1 (Gtr. I)

He stands, touch his hair, his shoes un-tied,

*Throughout Rhy. Fig. 1, play only lowest note of chord on beat 1.
Play all rhy. figs. w/slight variations ad lib when recalled (throughout).

w/Rhy. Fig. 1 (2½ times)

tongue-gap-ing stare.. Could I have been a mag-net for mon-ey? Could I have been

w/Rhy. Fill 1

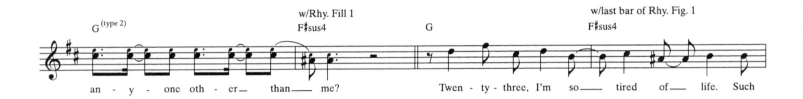

an-y-one oth-er than me? Twen-ty-three, I'm so tired of life. Such

w/Rhy. Fig. 1 (3 times)

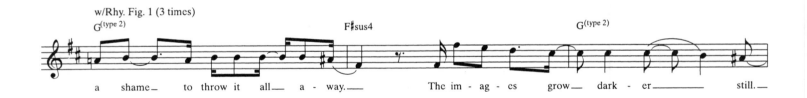

a shame to throw it all a-way. The im-ag-es grow dark-er still.

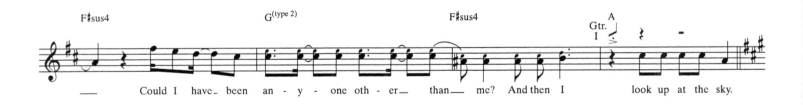

Could I have been an-y-one oth-er than me? And then I look up at the sky.

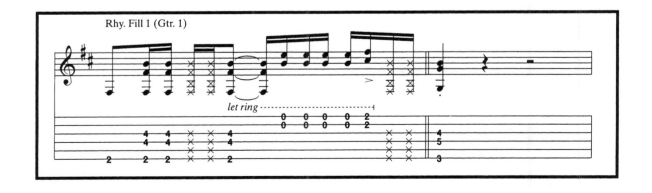

Rhy. Fill 1 (Gtr. 1)

let ring

DON'T DRINK THE WATER

Words and Music by
David J. Matthews

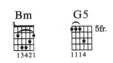

*Drop-D tuning:
⑥ = D

*All gtrs. except where otherwise indicated.

**Two acous. gtrs. arr. for one.

*Banjo arr. for gtr.
Open-D tuning (low to high): D A D F♯ A D

1st Verse
D5

Come out, come out, no use in hid - ing.

Riff A

*w/slide
let ring
w/o slide
w/slide
let ring
w/o slide
w/slide

Rhy. Fig. 2

*Wear slide on pinky.

w/Riff A (6 times)

(Gtr. I)

(end Rhy. Fig. 2)

*w/Rhy. Fig. 2 (3 times)

Come now, come now,—— can you not—— see?——

*Play all gtr. parts w/slight variations
ad lib when recalled (throughout).

There's no place here. What were you ex - pect - ing?

No room for both, just room for me.

54

w/slide - w/o slide

w/Rhy. Fig. 4
Bm

What's that___ you say?___ Your fa - ther's spir - it___ still

Riff C

G5

lives in___ this place? Well, I will si - lence you.___

w/Rhy. Fig. 1
D5

(cont. on upper staff)

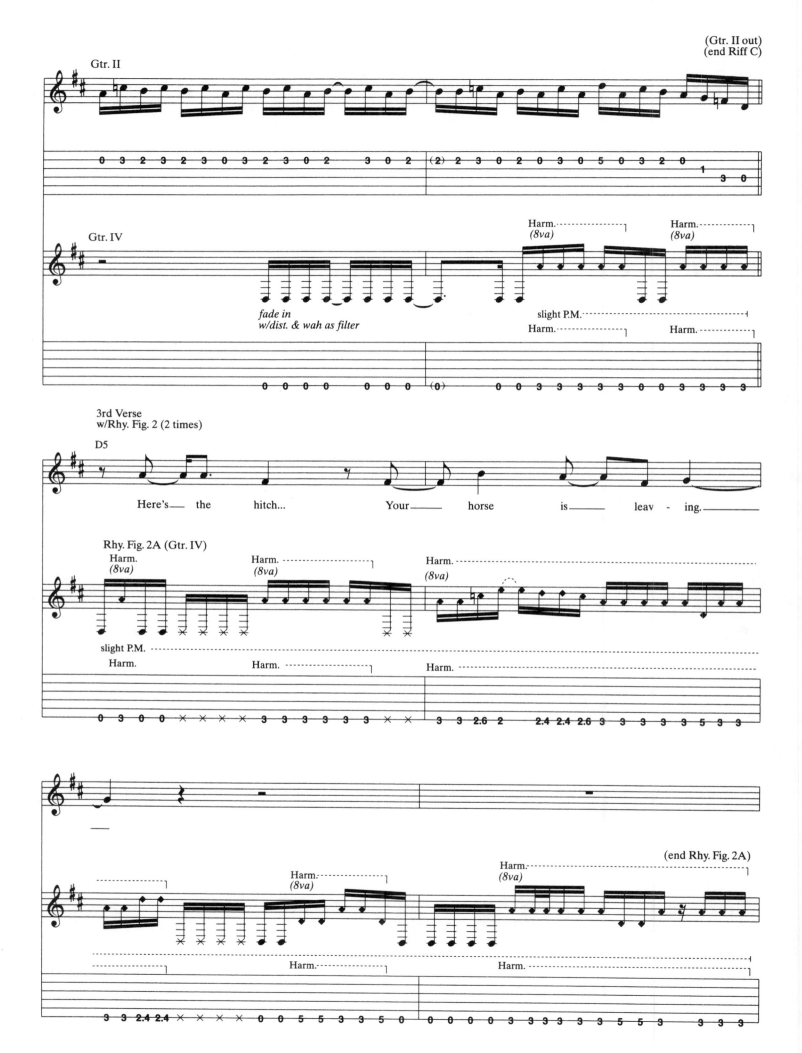

64

Segue to "Stay"

DREAMGIRL

Words and Music by
Dave Matthews Band and Mark Batson

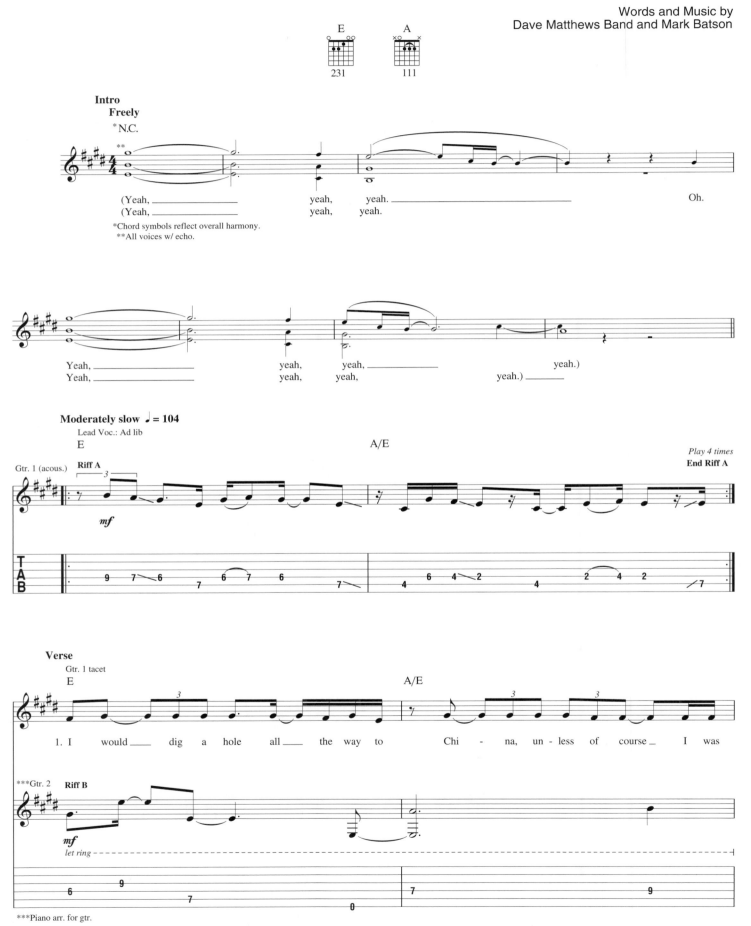

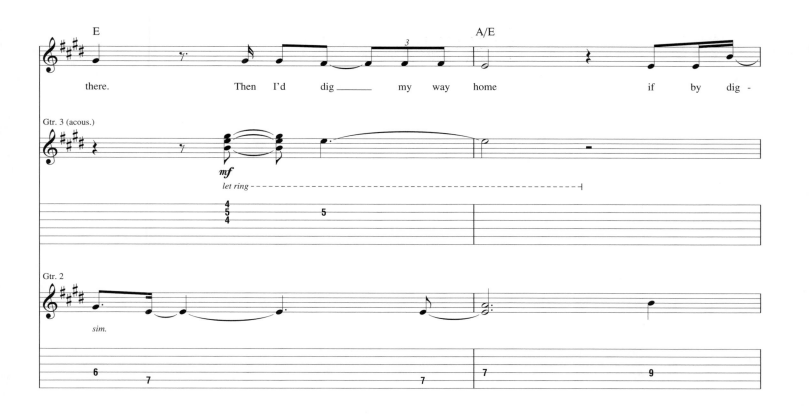

there. Then I'd dig ___ my way home if by dig-

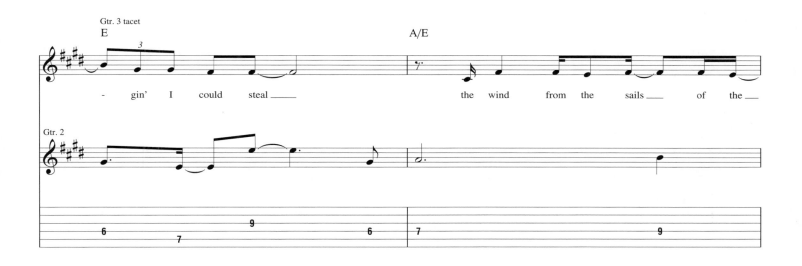

-gin' I could steal ___ the wind from the sails ___ of the ___

___ greed - y men who ___ rule ___ the world. ___ Still you're my best ___

End Riff B

Outro

EVERYDAY

Words and Music by
David J. Matthews and Glen Ballard

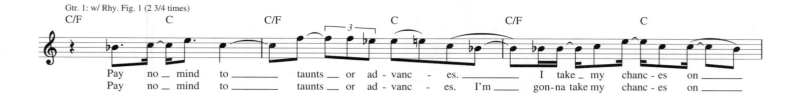

Pay no mind to _____ taunts __ or ad-vanc- es. _____ I take my chanc- es on _____
Pay no mind to _____ taunts __ or ad-vanc- es. I'm __ gon-na take my chanc- es on _____

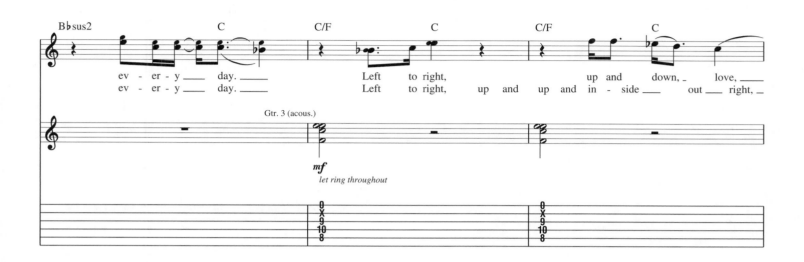

ev- er- y __ day. ____ Left to right, up and down, love, ____
ev- er- y __ day. ____ Left to right, up and up and in- side __ out __ right, __

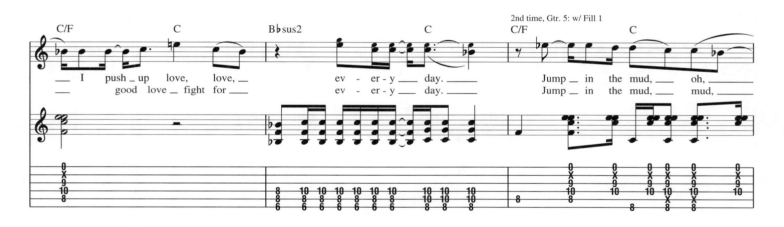

__ I push __ up love, love, __ ev- er- y __ day. ____ Jump __ in the mud, __ oh, __
good love __ fight for __ ev- er- y __ day. ____ Jump __ in the mud, __ mud, _____

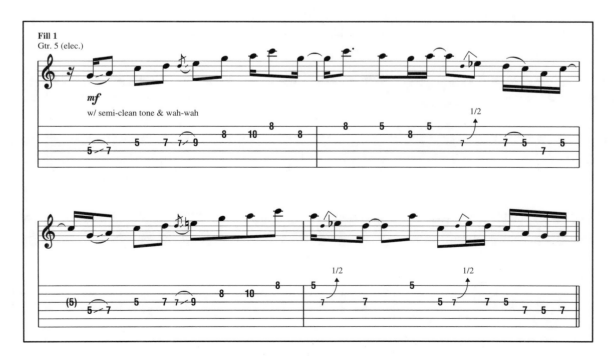

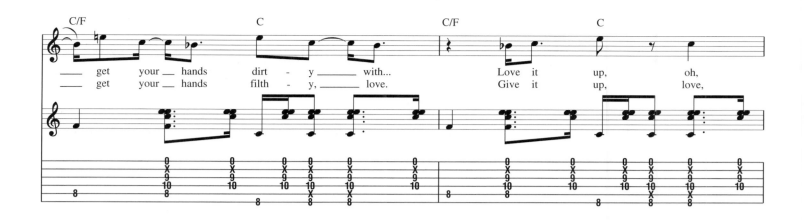

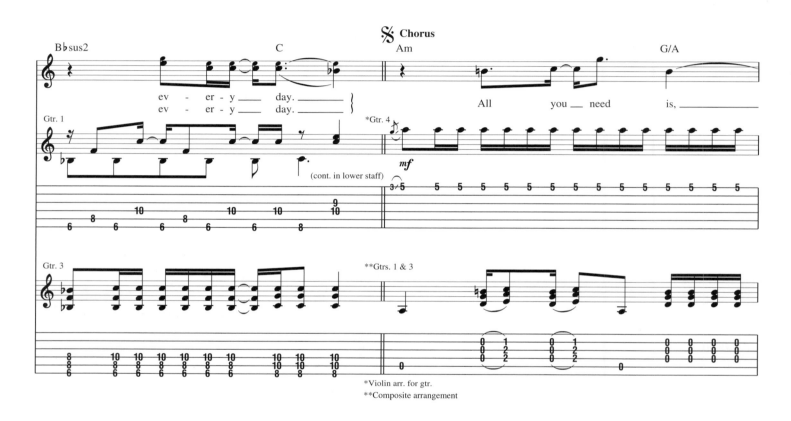

*Violin arr. for gtr.
**Composite arrangement

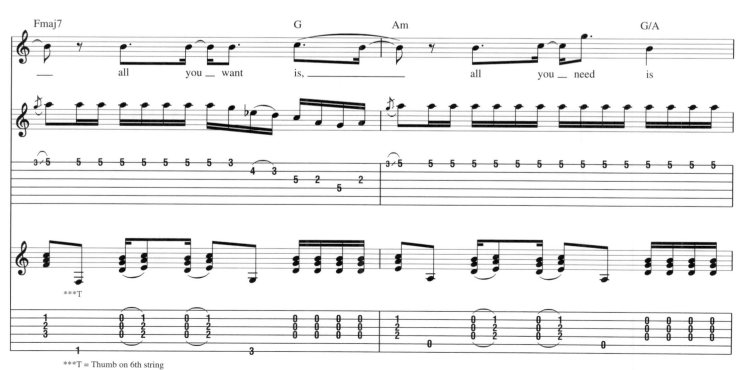

***T = Thumb on 6th string

74

*Last note of Rhy. Fig. 1 is played by Gtr. 1 only.

GRACE IS GONE

Lyrics by David J. Matthews
Music by Dave Matthews Band

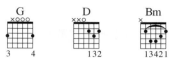

Gtr. 1: Open D tuning:
(low to high) D-A-D-F♯-A-D

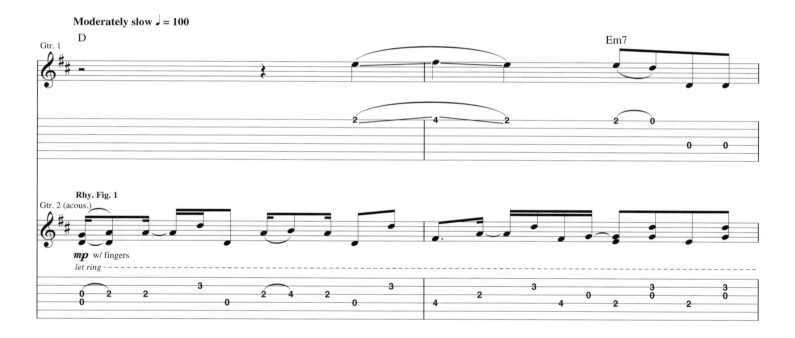

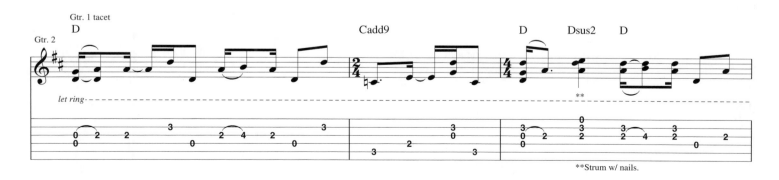

**Strum w/ nails.

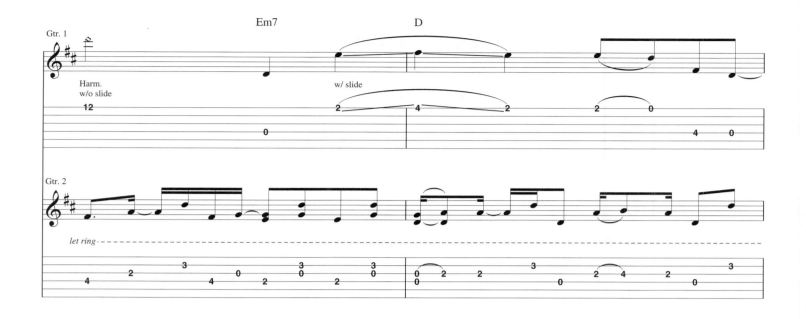

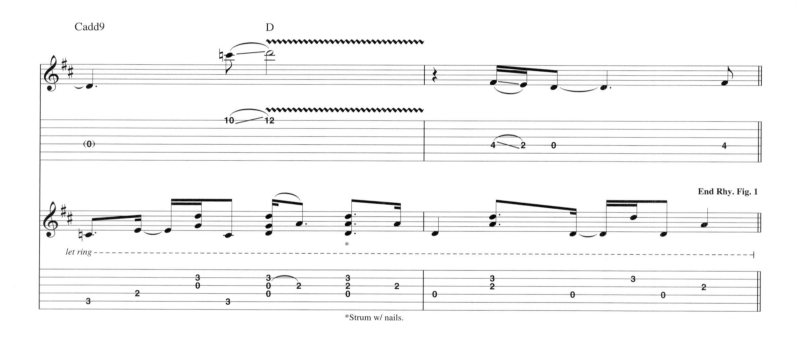

*Strum w/ nails.

Verse

1. Ne - on shines _____ through smok - y eyes _____ to - night. It's

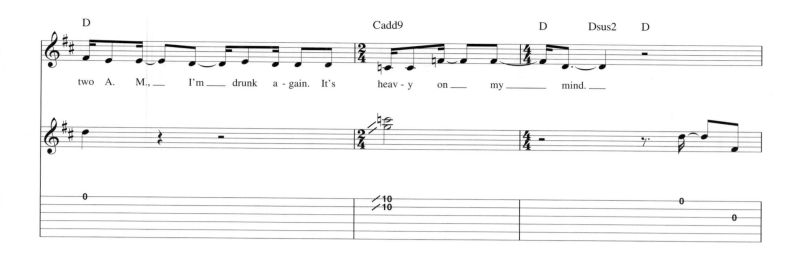

two A. M., __ I'm __ drunk a - gain. It's heav - y on __ my _____ mind.

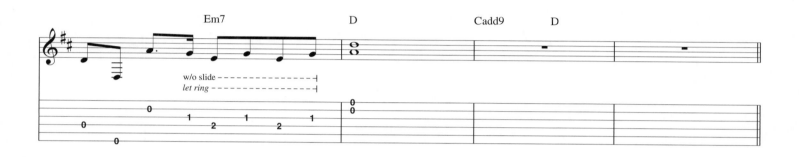

w/o slide - - - - - - - - - - - - - - - - -|
let ring - - - - - - - - - - - - - - - - -|

Verse
Gtr. 2: w/ Rhy. Fig. 1

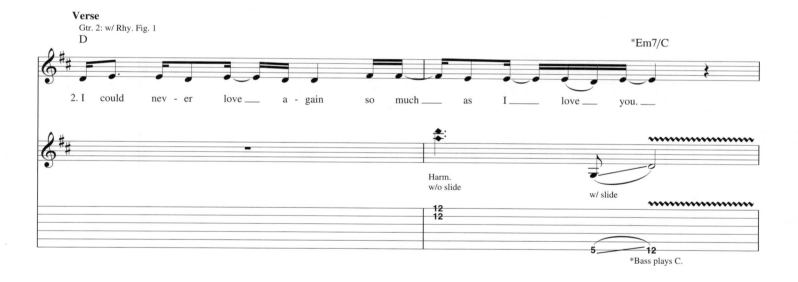

2. I could nev - er love __ a - gain so much __ as I __ love __ you. __

Harm.
w/o slide

w/ slide

*Bass plays C.

Where you end, __ where I __ be - gin, __ is like a _____ riv - er go - ing _____ through. __

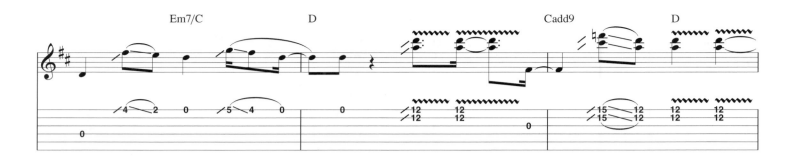

Verse

Gtr. 1 tacet

3. Take ___ my eyes, ___ take my ___ heart, I ___

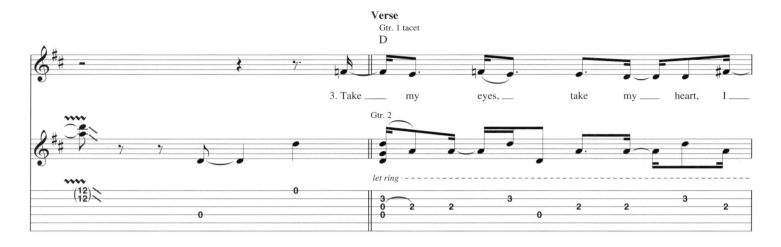

___ need them ___ no more ___ if nev-er a-gain ___ they fall ___ up-on ___ the

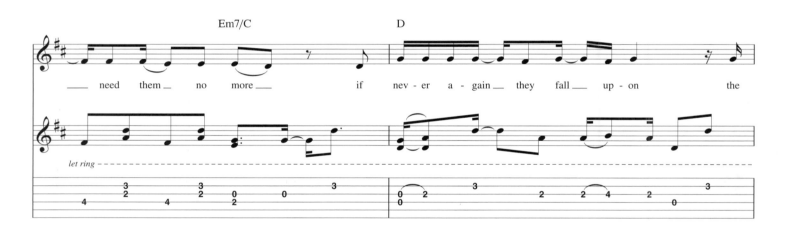

one I so ___ a - dore. ___ Ex - cuse ___ me, ___ please,

Chorus

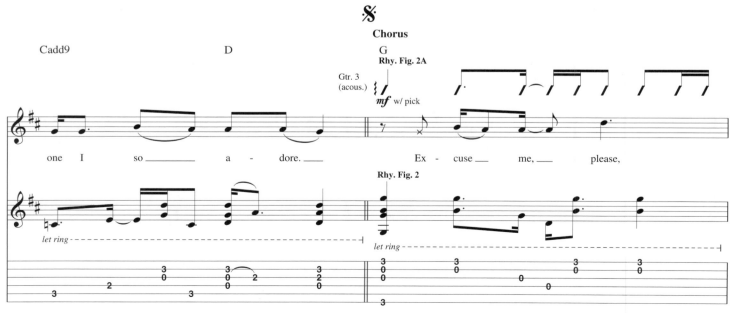

Interlude

*Strum w/ nails.

Verse

Gtr. 2: w/ Rhy. Fig. 1 (1st 4 meas.)
Gtr. 3 tacet

___ drink to re - mem - ber, ___ then an - oth - er to ___ for - get. Well, how ___

could I ev-er dream to find sweet love like you a-gain? _____ One _____

Gtr. 2

let ring -

*Strum w/ nails.

D.S. al Coda

drink to re-mem-ber and an-oth - er to _____ for - get. _____

let ring -

Coda

One _____ more drink _____ and I'll _____ be gone. _____

Rhy. Fig. 4

End Rhy. Fig. 4

let ring -

Rhy. Fig. 4A

End Rhy. Fig. 4A

Violin Solo

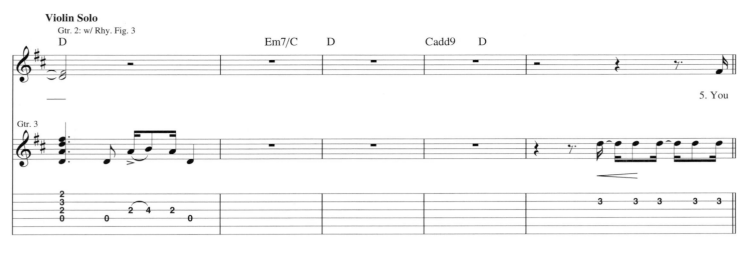

Verse

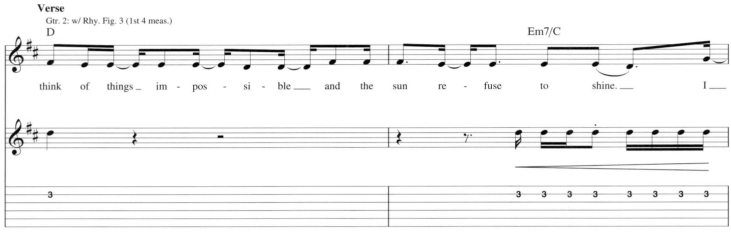

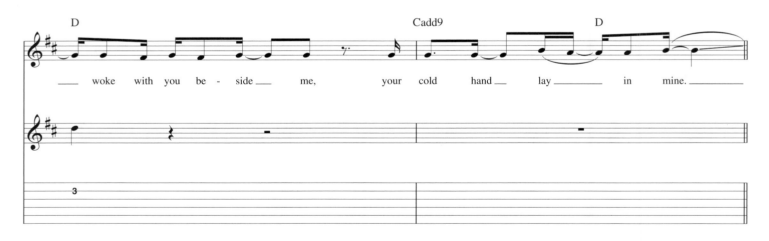

Chorus

GREY STREET

Lyrics by David J. Matthews
Music by Dave Matthews Band

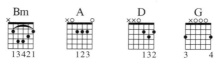

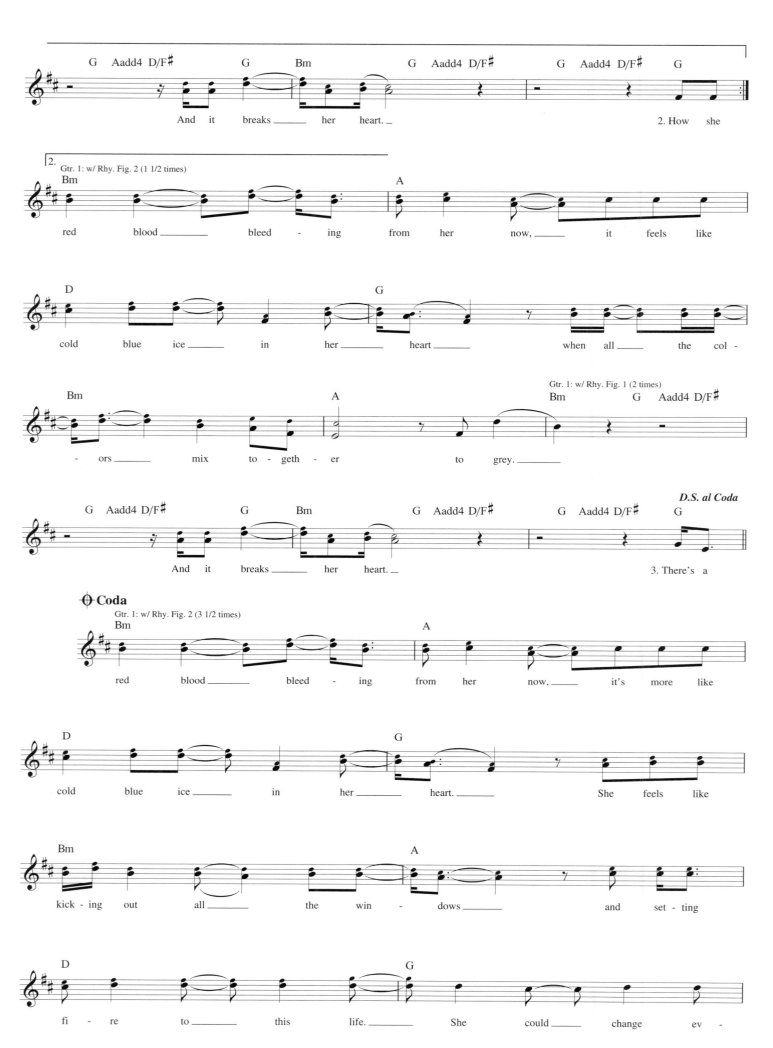

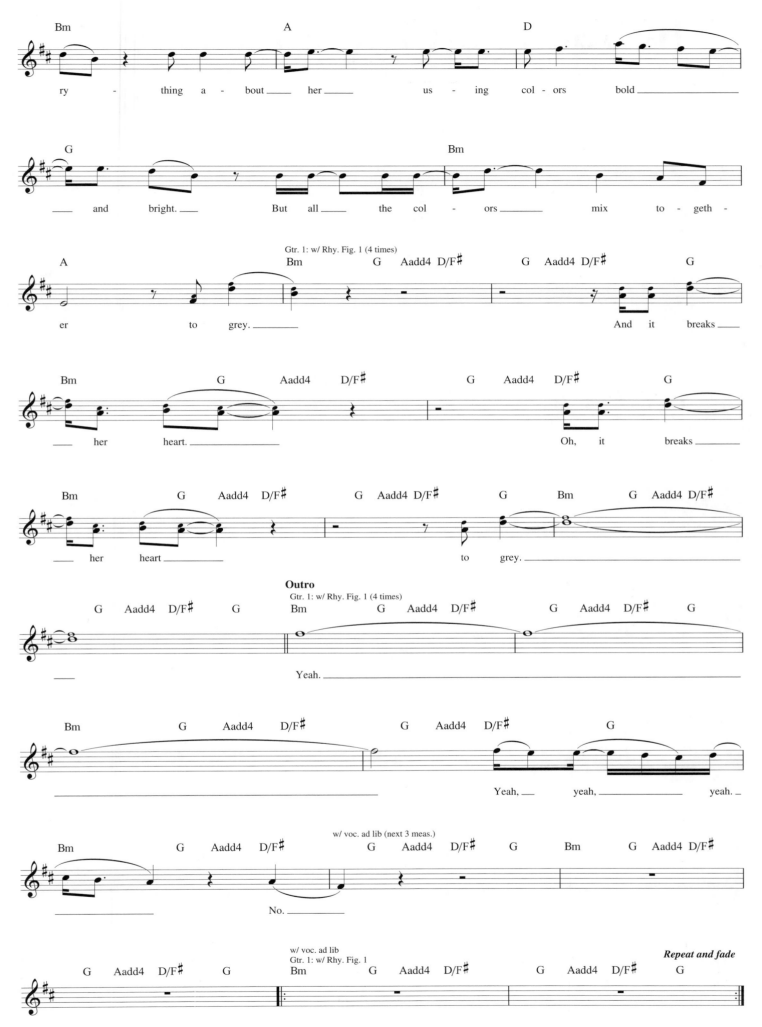

HUNGER FOR THE GREAT LIGHT

Words and Music by
Dave Matthews Band and Mark Batson

Coda 2

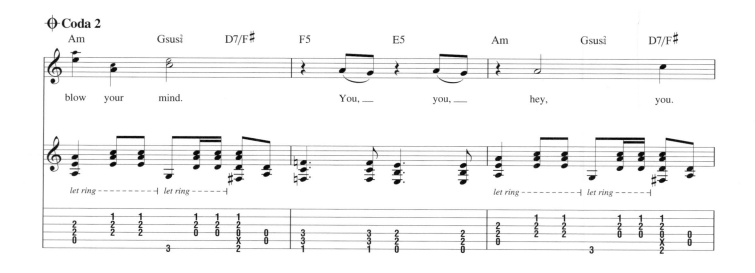

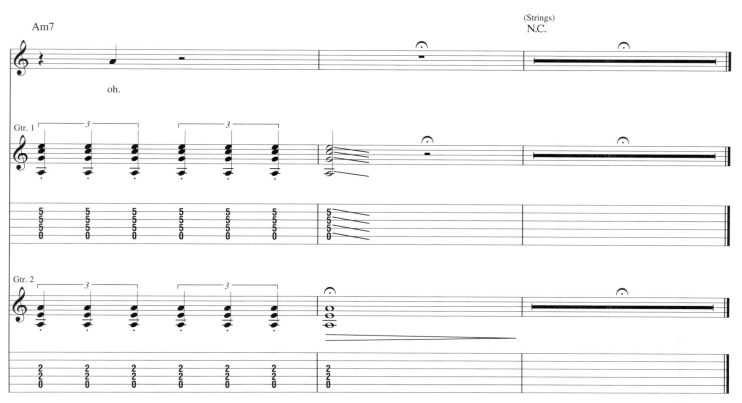

I DID IT

Words and Music by
David J. Matthews and Glen Ballard

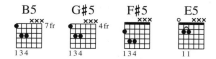

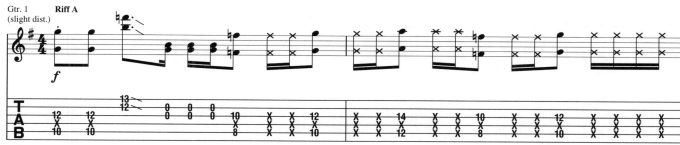

* Gtrs. 1 & 2: Tune down 2 1/2 steps:
(low to high) B–E–A–D–F#–B

Intro
Moderate Rock ♩ = 112

* Baritone gtrs. arr. for standard gtrs. (music sounds a 4th lower than indicated)

** Chord symbols reflect implied harmony.

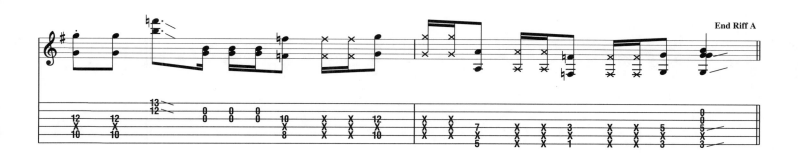

Verse

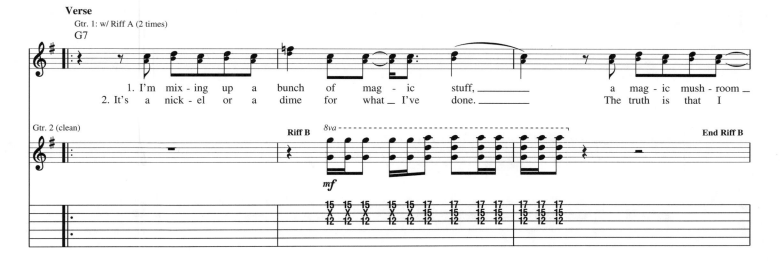

1. I'm mix-ing up a bunch of mag-ic stuff, ___ a mag-ic mush-room
2. It's a nick-el or a dime for what __ I've done. The truth is that I

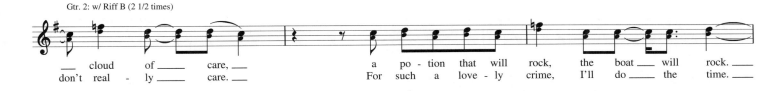

___ cloud of ___ care, a po-tion that will rock, the boat ___ will rock.
don't real-ly ___ care. ___ For such a love-ly crime, I'll do ___ the time.

Make a bomb of love and ___ blow ___ it up. ___
You bet - ter lock me up, I'll ___ do it a - gain. ___

Chorus

I did it. Do you think I've ___ gone ___ too far?

* Chord symbols reflect overall harmony.

I did it. Guilt - y ___ as ___ charged. I did it. ___ It was

me, right ___ or ___ wrong. I did it. Yeah. ___

Bridge

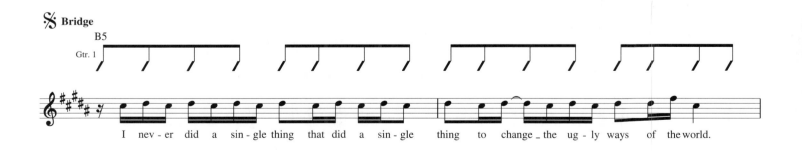

I nev - er did a sin - gle thing that did a sin - gle thing to change ___ the ug - ly ways of the world.

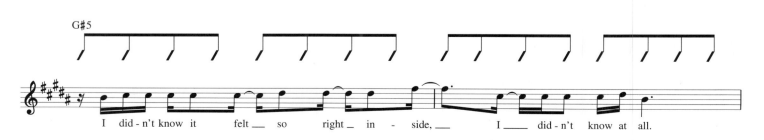

I did - n't know it felt ___ so right ___ in - side, ___ I ___ did - n't know at all.

F#5

I o-pen up the cur - tains, I __ heard si - rens there, _ the lights flash and crawl. __

1.

E5

But I did it jus - tice. I just did it for the buzz, _____ oh.

2.

E5

{ But I did it jus - tice. I just } did it for us all _____ you know.
{ But I did it jus - tice. Well, I }

Gtr. 1 N.C.   *Fine*

3. All you peo - ple are _____ the skew - ers of _____ our dreams, like the cat that col - lared _ me. __

Verse

Gtr. 1: w/ Riff A (2 times)   Gtr. 2: w/ Riff B (3 1/2 times)

G7

Spoken:
__ Oh, what I got - ta say to you. You got love, don't turn it down. _ Turn it

loud, let it build. We got a long way to go, but you, you got - ta _____ start _____ some-where.

Verse

Gtr. 1: w/ Riff A (2 times)
Gtr. 2: w/ Riff B (2nd meas.)

Gtr. 2: w/ Riff B (3 1/2 times)

G7

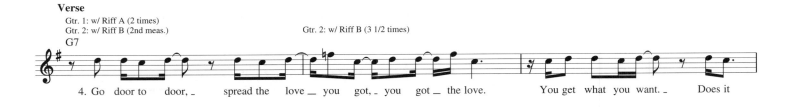

4. Go door to door, __ spread the love __ you got, __ you got __ the love. You get what you want. __ Does it

mat-ter where you get it from? I for one __ don't turn ___ my cheek for an-y-one. __

Chorus

Gtr. 1: w/ Rhy. Fig. 1 (8 times)

N.C.   D7   D6

Un-turn your ___ cheek to give your love, love to grow. _____ I did it. Do you

D   Dsus4   D5   D6   N.C.   D7   D6   D   Dsus4/E   D/F♯ D6

think I've __ gone __ too far? I did it. Guilt-y __ as ___ charged.

N.C.   D7   D6   D   Dsus4   D5   D6   N.C.   D7   D6

I did it. ___ It was me, right or ___ wrong. ___ I did it.

D   Dsus4/E   D/F♯ D6   N.C.   D7   D6   D   Dsus4/E   D/F♯   D6

Yeah, __ yeah, __ yeah. ___ I did it. I told you, I ___ told you, I did. ___

N.C.   D7   D6   D   Dsus4/E   D/F♯ D6   N.C.   D7   D6

I did it. Guilt-y ___ as ___ charged. I did it. I

D.S. al Fine
(take 2nd ending)

D   Dsus4/E   D/F♯ D6   N.C.   D7   D6   D   Dsus4/E D/F♯ D6

told you, I ___ told you, I did. ___ I did it. Yeah. ___

JIMI THING

Words and Music by
David J. Matthews

_____ to some-thing bet - ter._____ What_ I_ want_ is what I've

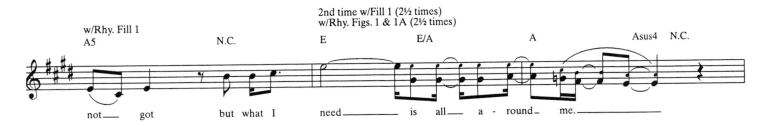

not_ got but what I need_ is all_ a - round_ me._____

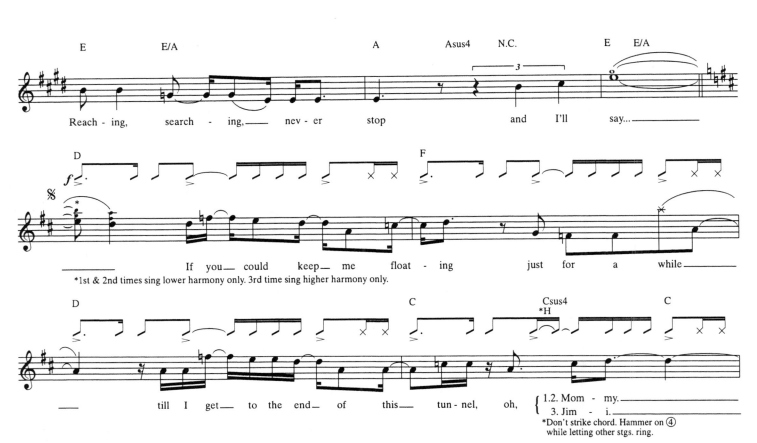

Reach - ing, search - ing,_____ nev - er stop and I'll say..._____

_____ If you_ could keep_ me float - ing just for a while_____

*1st & 2nd times sing lower harmony only. 3rd time sing higher harmony only.

_____ till I get_ to the end_ of this_ tun - nel, oh, { 1.2. Mom - my._____
{ 3. Jim - i.

*Don't strike chord. Hammer on ④
while letting other stgs. ring.

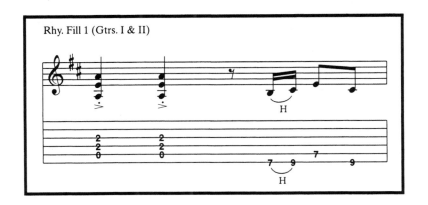

Rhy. Fill 1 (Gtrs. I & II)

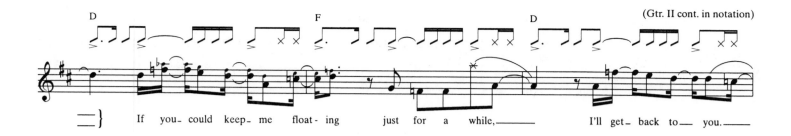

If you could keep me float-ing just for a while,_____ I'll get back to__ you.__

If you could keep me float-ing just for a while,_____ I'll get back to__ you.__

—

1. Some - time a Jim - i_____ thing
2.3. Some - time__ I take a Jim - i thing,_____

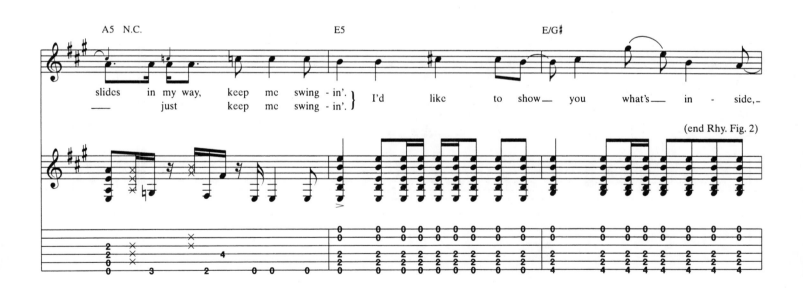

slides in my way, keep me swing - in'. } I'd like to show__ you what's__ in - side,—
—— just keep me swing - in'.

but I should - n't care____ if you don't__ like__ it. Broth - er____ cha - os

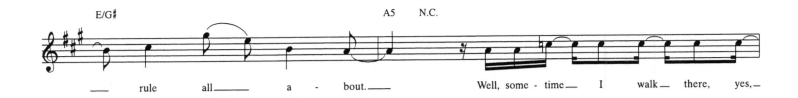

rule all a - bout. Well, some - time I walk there, yes,

God knows some - time I take a bus there. Should - n't care, I should - n't care, be - reaved

as I'm feel - in'.

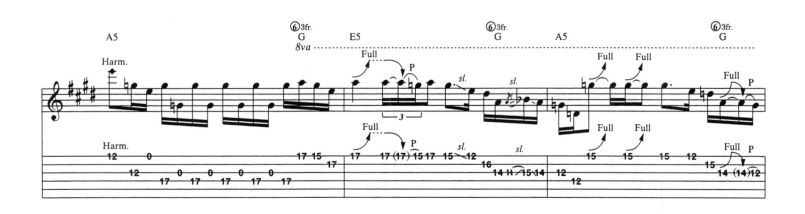

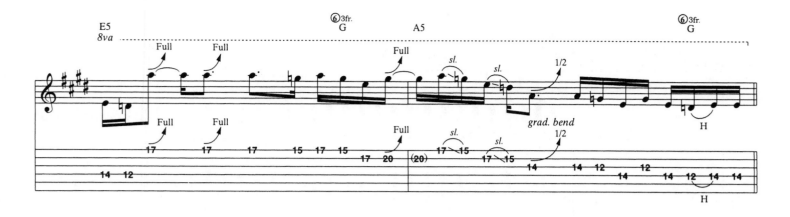

w/Rhy. Figs. 1 & 1A (2 times)

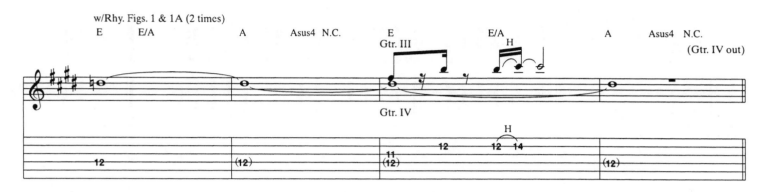

w/Rhy. Figs. 1 & 1A (3½ times) and Fill 2 (3 times)

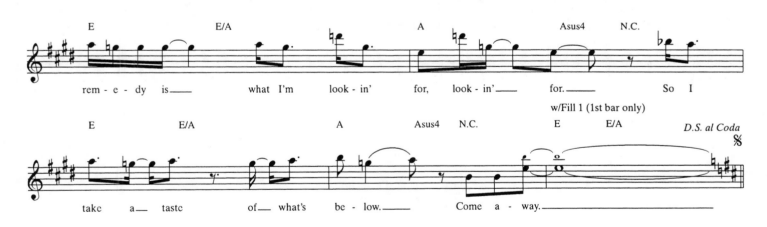

Late - ly I've _____ been feel - in' low. _____ Well, the

rem - e - dy is _____ what I'm look - in' for, look - in' _____ for. _____ So I

take a _____ taste of _____ what's be - low. _____ Come a - way.

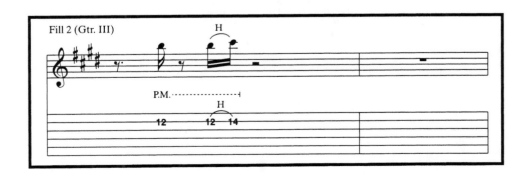

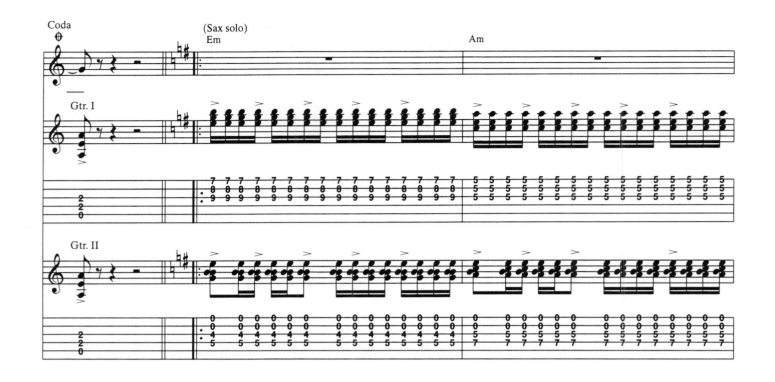

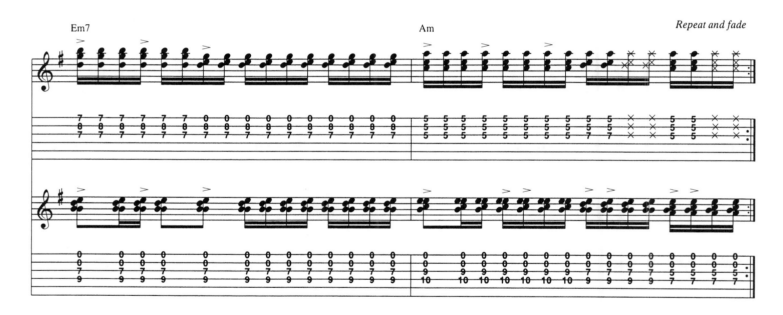

Additional Lyrics

2. The day is gone, I'm on my back
   Starin' up at the ceiling.
   I take a drink, sit back and relax.
   Smoke my mind to make me feel better for a small time.
   What I want is what I've not got
   And what I need is all around me.
   Reachin', searchin', never stop.
   And I'll say...
   If you keep me floating, *etc.*

LOUISIANA BAYOU

Words and Music by
Dave Matthews Band and Mark Batson

Verse

Gtr. 1: w/ Riff B (2 times)
Gtr. 3 tacet

Gtr. 3: w/ Riff B1

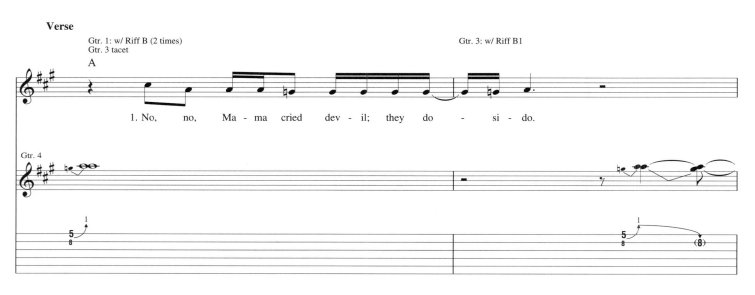

1. No, no, Ma - ma cried dev - il; they do - si - do.

Gtr. 4

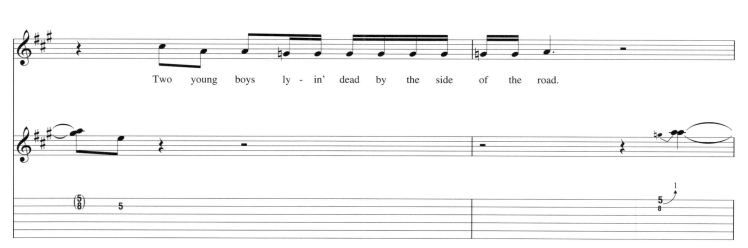

Two young boys ly - in' dead by the side of the road.

And the coins on their eyes rep - re - sent the mon - ey they owe.

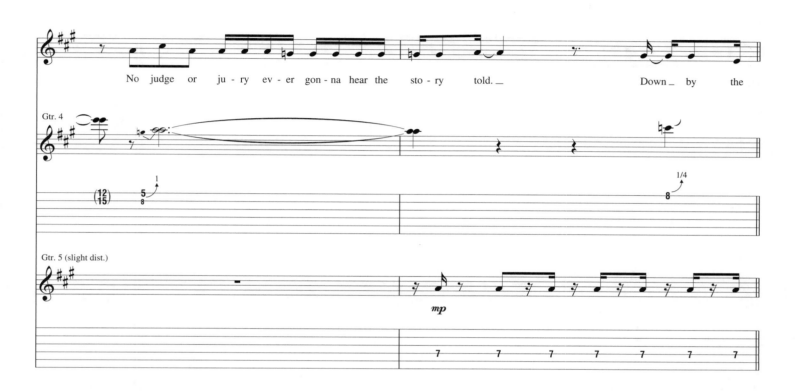

No judge or ju - ry ev - er gon - na hear the sto - ry told. __ Down __ by the

Chorus

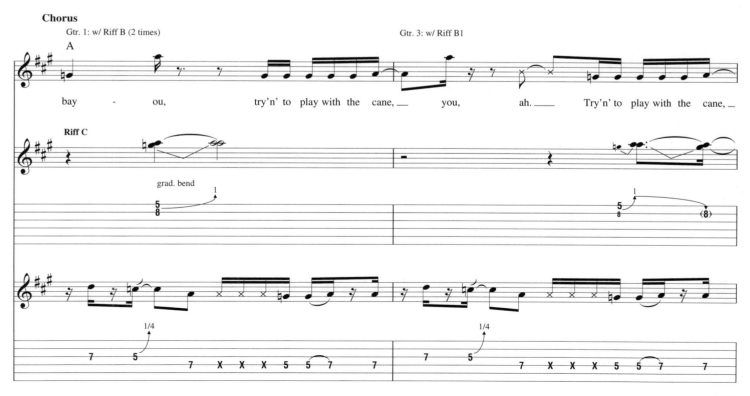

bay - ou, try'n' to play with the cane, __ you, ah. ___ Try'n' to play with the cane, __

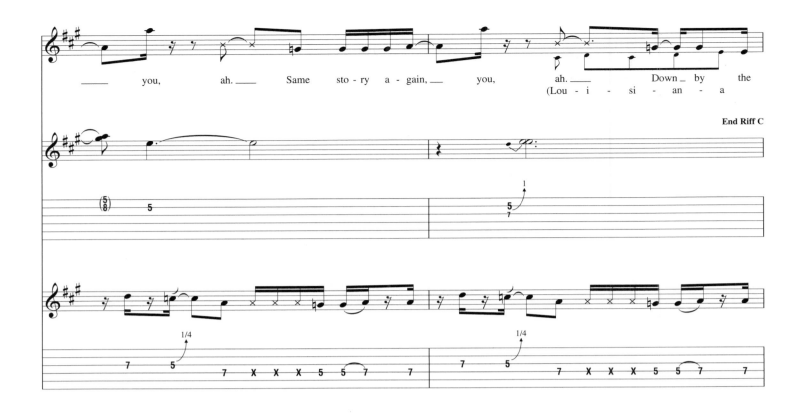

*Harp harmonics achieved by lightly touching string w/ index finger at fret indicated in parentheses and picking from behind.

you, ah. ___ Same sto-ry a-gain, ___ you, ah. (Lou - i - si - an - a

Gtr. 2: w/ Riff A (2 times)
Gtr. 3: w/ Riff B1

Bay - ou.
bay - ou.)

Gtr. 1

Gtr. 4

Gtr. 6

Pitch: D   B   G   D

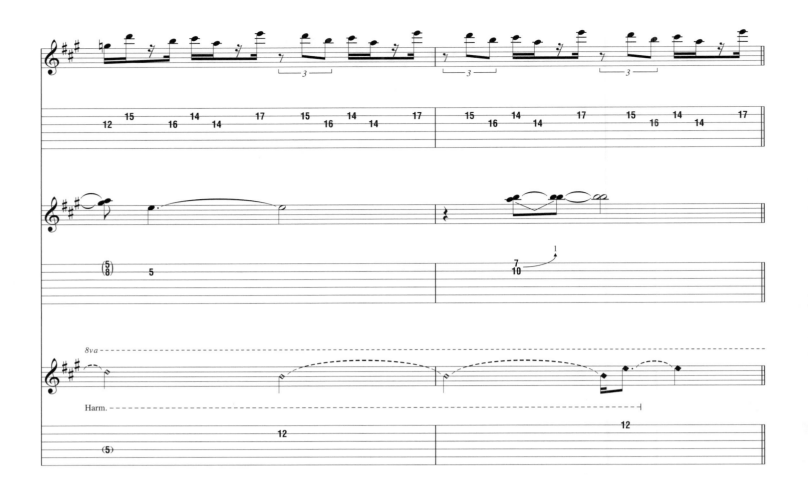

%S Verse

Gtr. 1: w/ Riff B (2 times)
2nd time, Gtr. 4: w/ Riff C (2 times)
2nd time, Gtr. 6 tacet (next 8 meas.)

Gtr. 3: w/ Riff B1

2. Sweet girl, Dad - dy done beat that girl like he's in - sane.
3. Mon - ey on my bed, but you ain't got _____ to go.

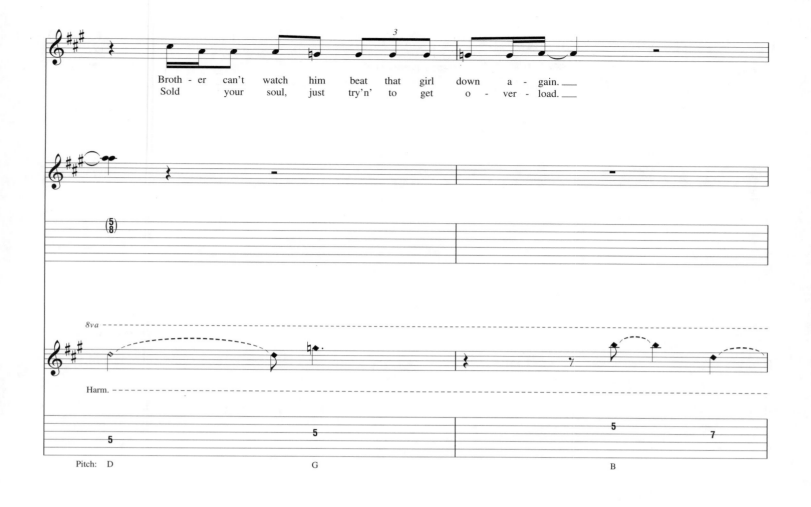

Broth - er can't watch him beat that girl down a - gain. ___
Sold your soul, just try'n' to get o - ver - load. ___

Pitch: D   G   B

Gtr. 3: w/ Riff B1

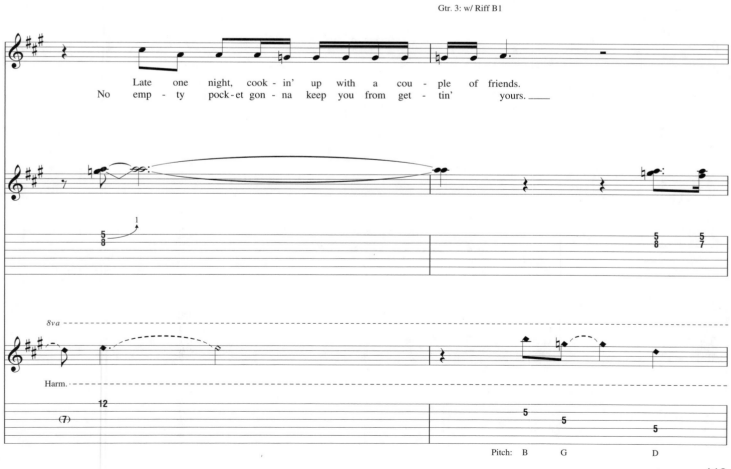

Late one night, cook - in' up with a cou - ple of friends.
No emp - ty pock-et gon - na keep you from get - tin' yours. ___

Pitch: B   G   D

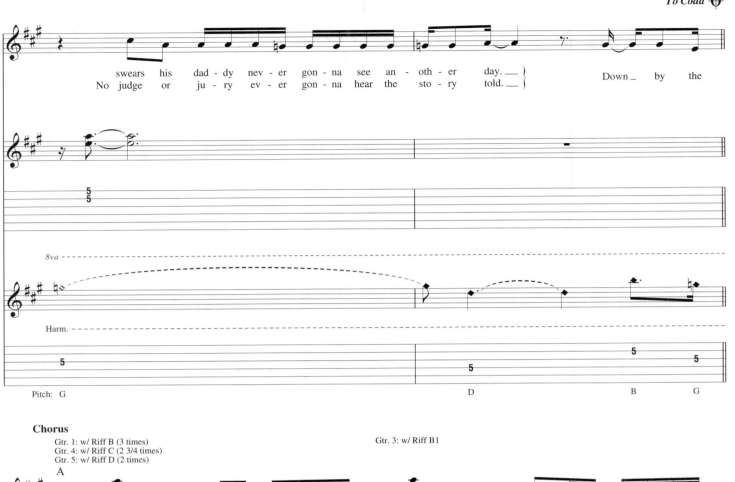

swears his dad - dy nev - er gon - na see an - oth - er day. ___
No judge or ju - ry ev - er gon - na hear the sto - ry told. ___
Down ___ by the

Pitch: G   D   B   G

Chorus

Gtr. 1: w/ Riff B (3 times)
Gtr. 4: w/ Riff C (2 3/4 times)
Gtr. 5: w/ Riff D (2 times)

Gtr. 3: w/ Riff B1

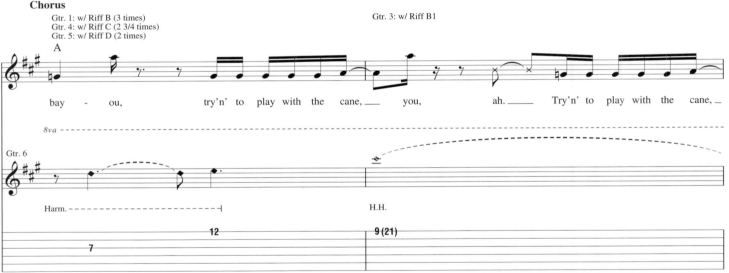

bay - ou,   try'n' to play with the cane, ___ you,   ah. ___   Try'n' to play with the cane, ___

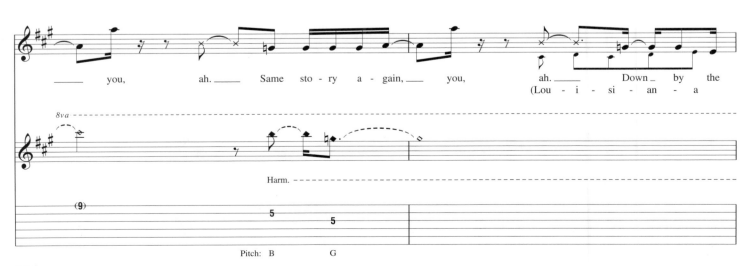

___ you,   ah. ___ Same sto - ry a - gain, ___ you,   ah. ___   Down by the
(Lou - i - si - an - a

Pitch: B   G

114

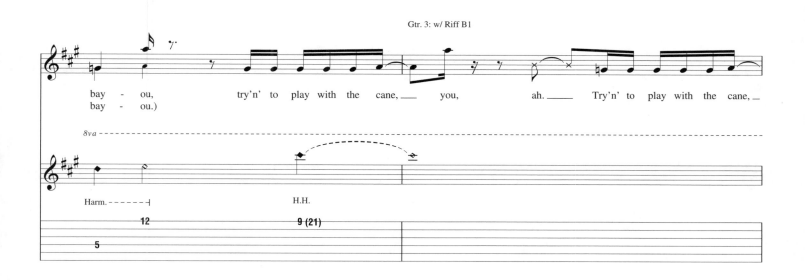

bay - ou, try'n' to play with the cane, ___ you, ah. ___ Try'n' to play with the cane, ___
bay - ou.)

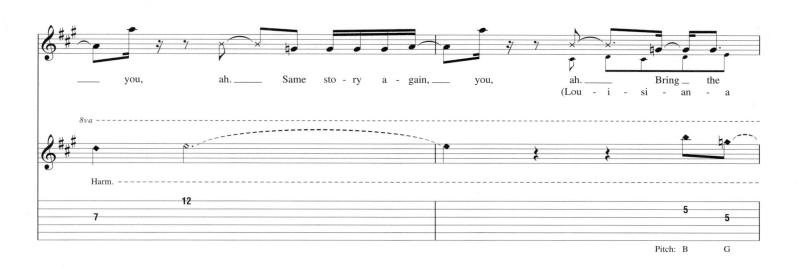

___ you, ah. ___ Same sto - ry a - gain, ___ you, ah. ___ Bring ___ the
(Lou - i - si - an - a

Pitch: B   G

same. No, no, Ma - ma cried dev - il; they do - si - do.
bay - ou.)

Pitch: D

See two young boys ly - in' dead by the side of the road. Shame, ___

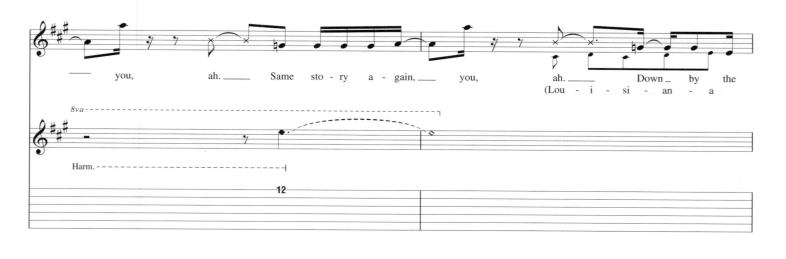

you, ah. Same sto - ry a - gain, you, ah. Down by the
(Lou - i - si - an - a

Gtr. 6 tacet   Gtr. 3: w/ Riff B1

bay - ou, try'n' to play with the cane, you, ah. Try'n' to play with the cane,
bay - ou.)

you, ah. Same sto - ry a - gain, you, ah.
(Lou - i - si - an - a

Gtr. 5: w/ Riff D (1st 2 meas., 2 times)   Gtr. 3: w/ Riff B1

No, no, Ma - ma cried dev - il; they do - si - do.
bay - ou.)

Gtr. 6

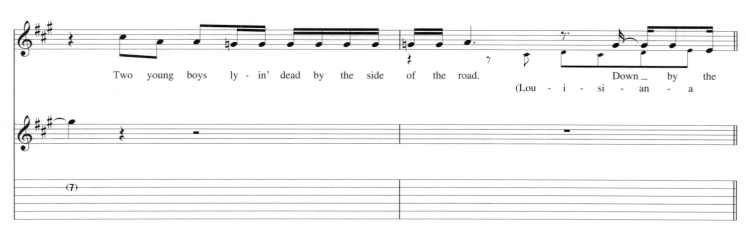

Two young boys ly - in' dead by the side of the road. Down by the
(Lou - i - si - an - a

Outro

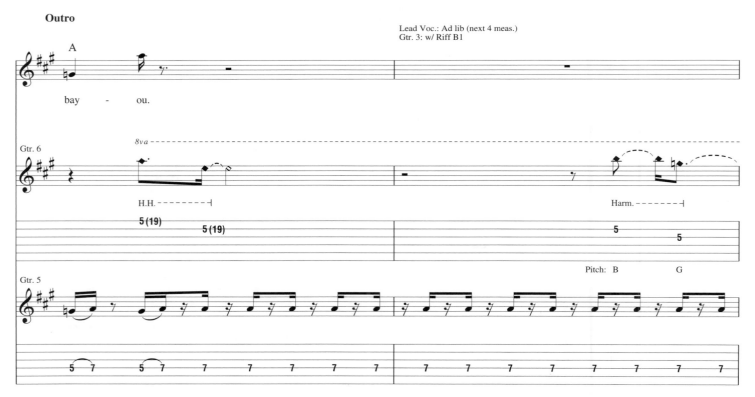

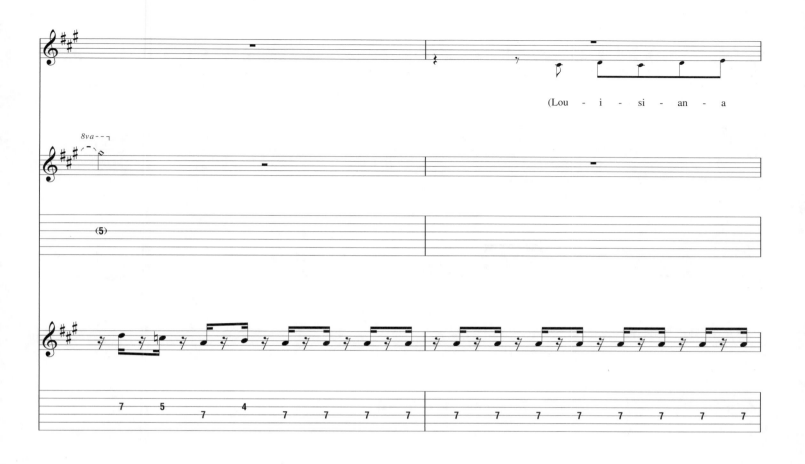

(Lou - i - si - an - a

Gtr. 3: w/ Riff B1

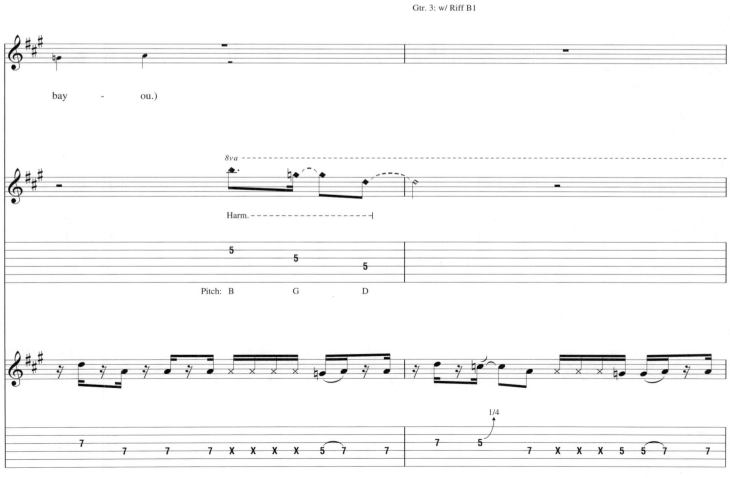

bay - ou.)

Pitch: B   G   D

(Lou - i - si - an - a

bay - ou.)

Gtr. 6 tacet

Gtr. 5

Gtr. 3: w/ Riff B1

Gtr. 3: w/ Riff B1

A

Repeat and fade

122

RAPUNZEL

Words and Music by David J. Matthews,
Stefan Lessard and Carter Beauford

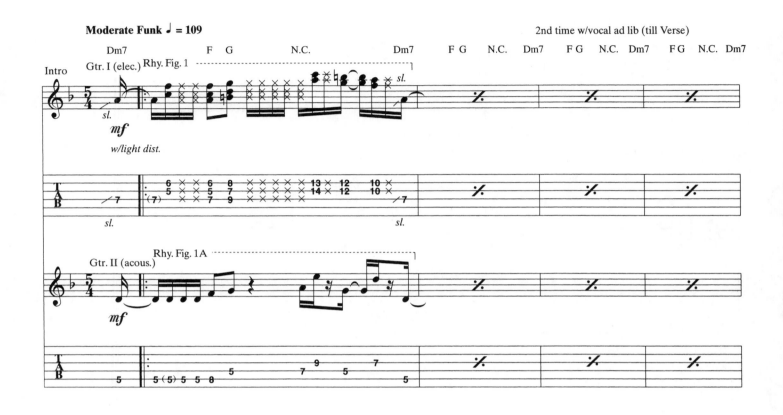

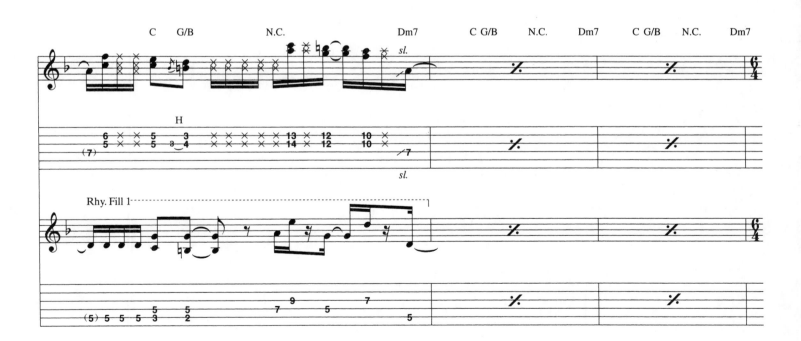

2nd time Gtr. I substitute Rhy. Fill 4

Rhy. Fill 4 (Gtr. I)

that I'll— do my best——— for— you, I do.—
that I'll— do my best——— for— you, I do.—

(end Rhy. Fig. 2)   Rhy. Fill 3 -----------------------------------

w/Rhy. Fig. 2
2nd time Gtr. I substitute Rhy. Fill 5

Love,— let's stop to get it go in'. Lost— my self— just think -
Oh,— for— you I would crawl— through— the dark - est dun -

Gtr. I

Rhy. Fill 5 (Gtr. I)

126

*Substitute muted strings in parentheses when recalled.

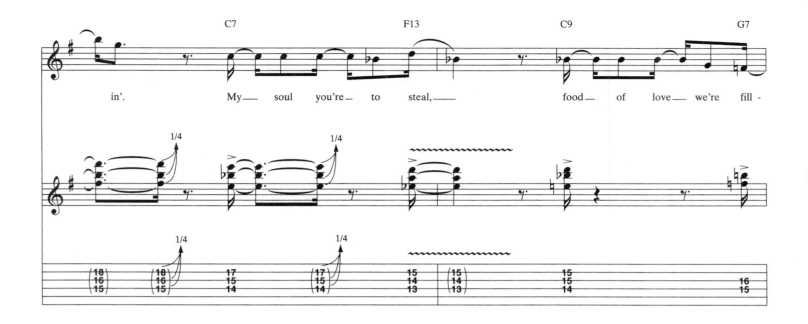

in'. My soul you're to steal, food of love we're fill-

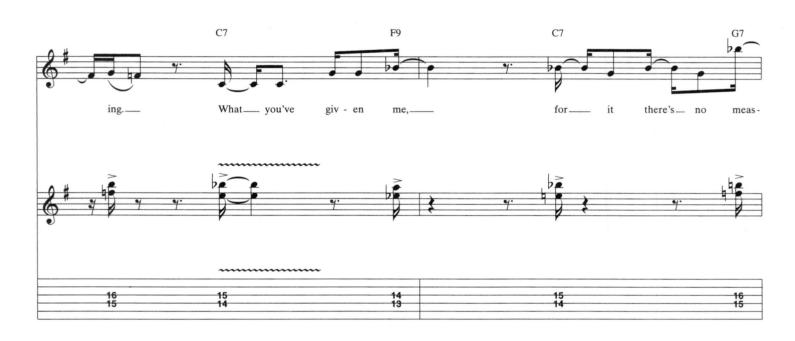

ing. What you've giv-en me, for it there's no meas-

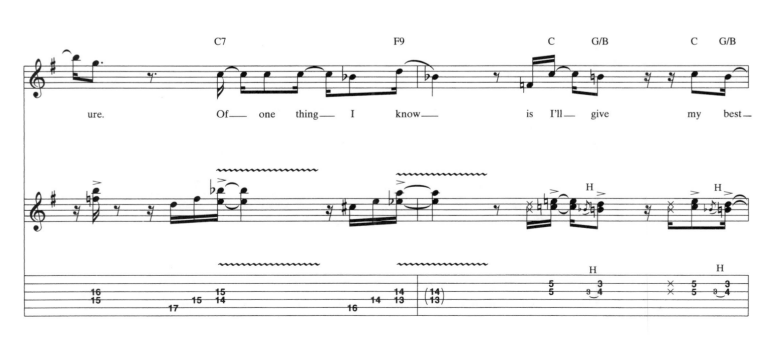

ure. Of one thing I know is I'll give my best

131

with—— you look-ing at—— me.   You—— make me—— feel high.——

With ev - 'ry sin - gle thing—— you do—— to me is like—— I'm drunk.——

w/Rhy. Fill 3

—— I—— do my best—— for—— you,   I do.——

Outro

w/voc. ad lib (next 6 bars)

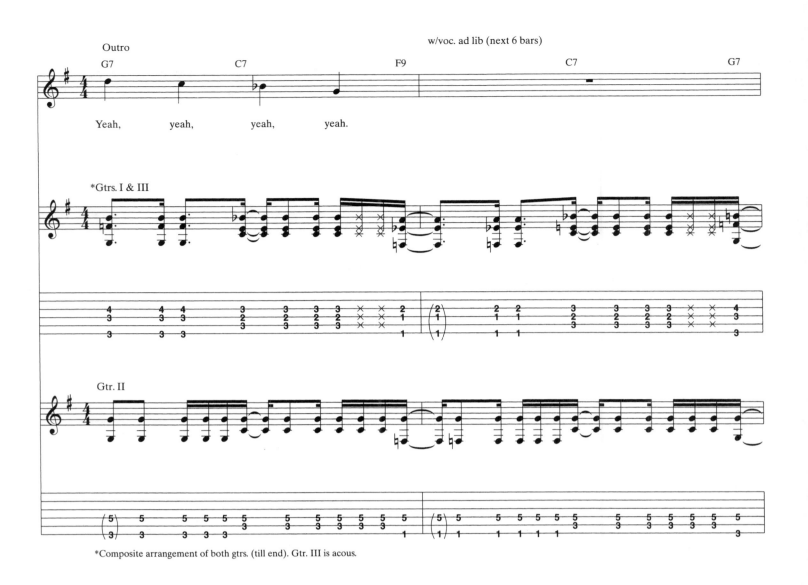

Yeah,   yeah,   yeah,   yeah.

*Composite arrangement of both gtrs. (till end). Gtr. III is acous.

*Play w/variations ad lib when recalled.

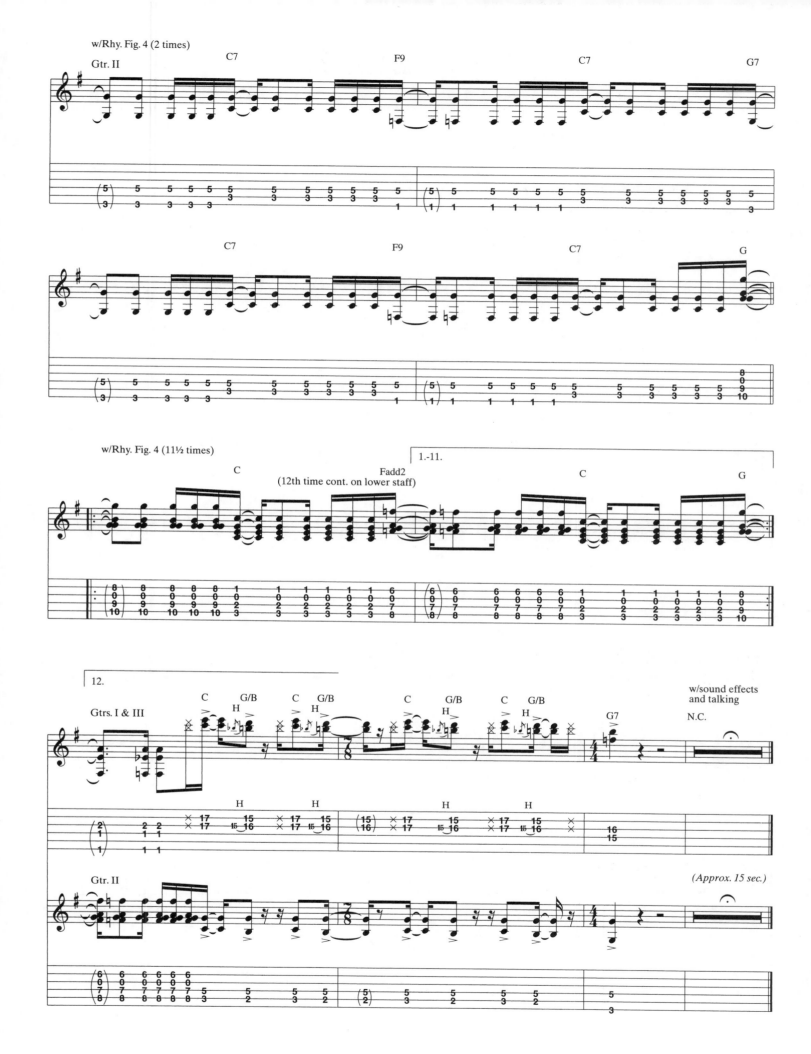

SATELLITE

Words and Music by
David J. Matthews

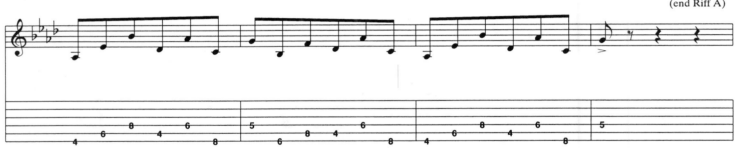

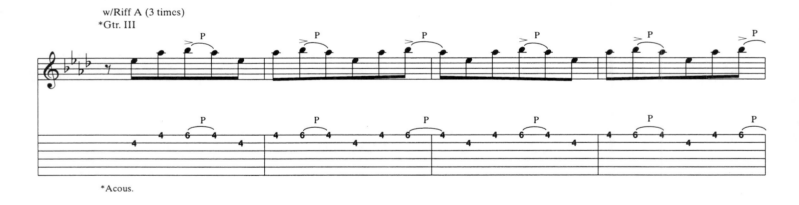

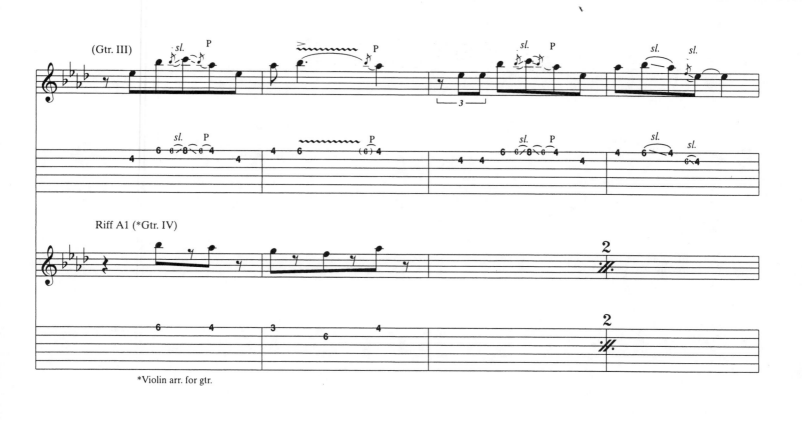

*Violin arr. for gtr.

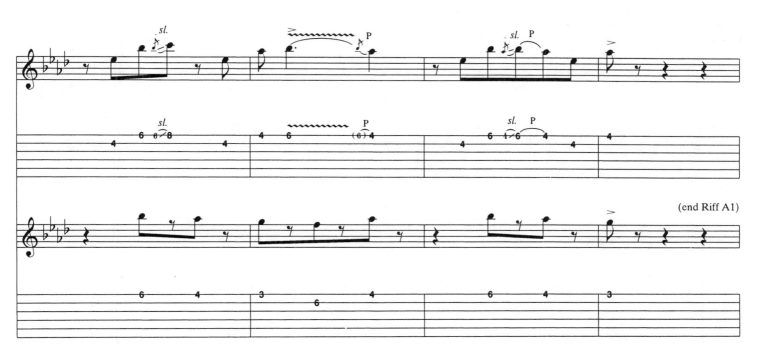

1. Sat - el -

(Gtr. III out)

1st, 2nd, 3rd Verses
w/Riff A (1¾ times)
2nd time w/Riff A1 (1¾ times) & Riff B
3rd time w/Riff A1 (1 time only)

N.C.

(1.3.) lite in my eyes,_____ like a dia - mond in the sky.
(2.) lite head - lines read._____ Some - one's se - crets you've seen, eyes__ and

*Harmony is sung 3rd time only.

How I won - der. Sat - el - lite strong__ from__ the moon,__
cars__ have been. Sat - el - lite dish__ in__ my yard,__

and the world your__ bal - loon. Peep - ing__ Tom__ for the__
tell me more, tell__ me__ more. Who's__ the__ king__ of your__

Riff B (*Gtr. V)   Play 3 times

w/slide

*Acous.

Play 3 times   (Gtr. V out)

*Vib. w/slide.

138

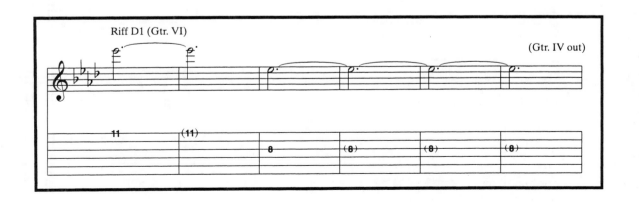

SAY GOODBYE

Words and Music by
David J. Matthews

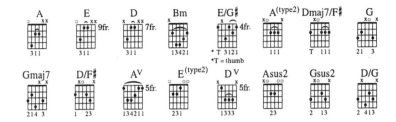

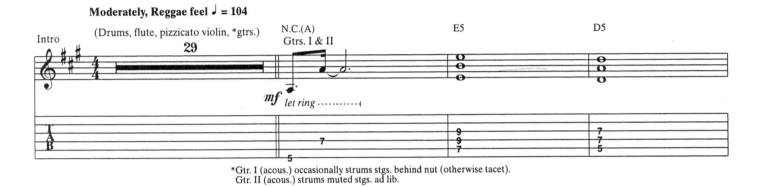

*Gtr. I (acous.) occasionally strums stgs. behind nut (otherwise tacet).
Gtr. II (acous.) strums muted stgs. ad lib.

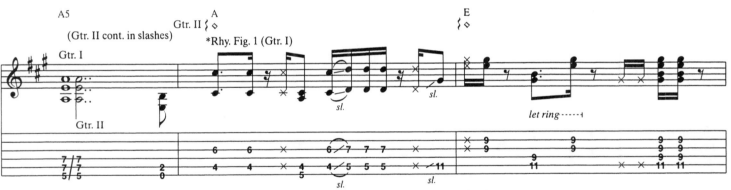

*Play all rhy. figs. w/slight variations ad lib when recalled (throughout).

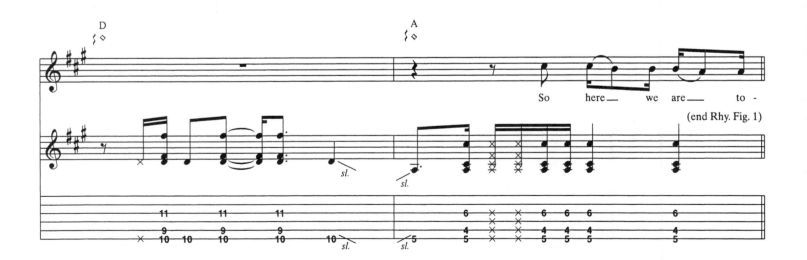

So here____ we are____ to-
(end Rhy. Fig. 1)

night, you and me to-geth-er_____ with the storm____ out-

side and the fi-re's bright. Oh,____ and in your

w/Rhy. Figs. 2 & 2A (both 3 times)

eyes I see____ what's on____ my____ mind.____ And you got__ me wild,__

__ turned a-round in - side.____ Oh,__ and then__ de-si -

re, see,__ is creep-ing up heav-y, ah, in - side

SO MUCH TO SAY

Words and Music by David J. Matthews,
Boyd Tinsley and Peter Griesar

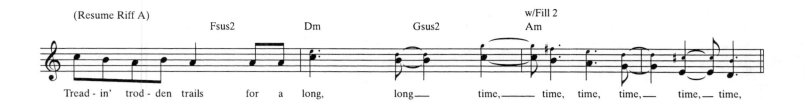

(Resume Riff A)

Fsus2 Dm Gsus2 Am w/Fill 2

Tread - in' trod - den trails for a long, long— time,— time, time, time,— time,— time,

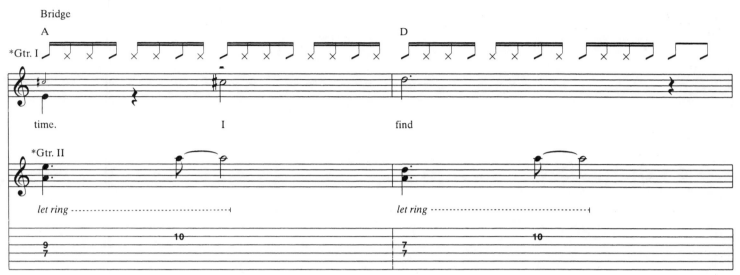

Bridge

A   D

*Gtr. I

time.   I   find

*Gtr. II

let ring ------------------┤ let ring ------------------┤

* 2nd time both gtrs. play w/slight variations ad lib.

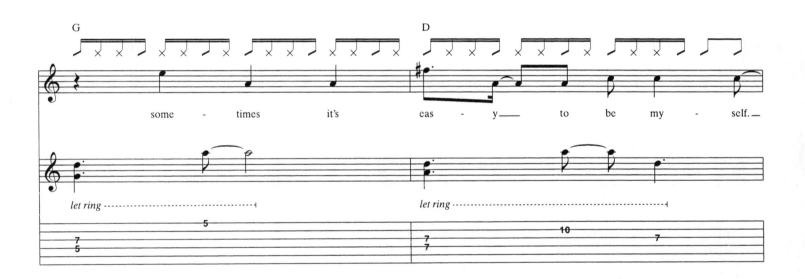

G   D

some - times it's eas - y— to be my - self.—

let ring ------------------┤ let ring ------------------┤

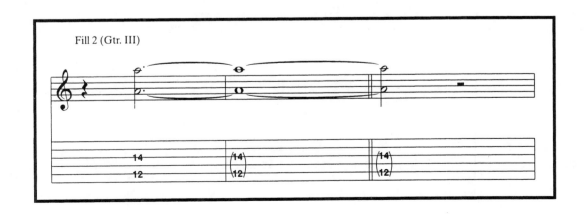

Fill 2 (Gtr. III)

155

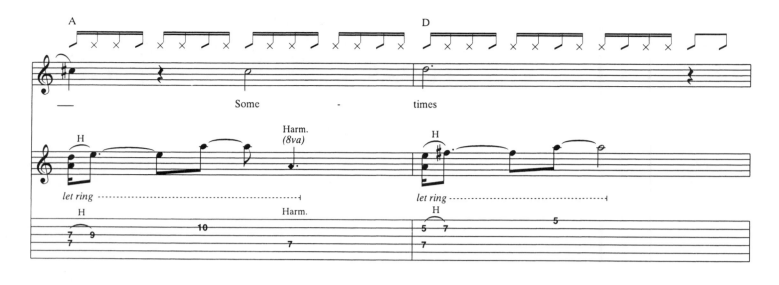

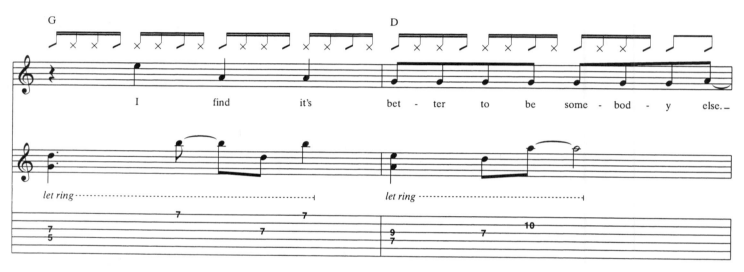

w/Rhy. Fig. 1 and *Riff A (both last 2 bars only)
w/Fill 1

3rd Verse
w/Rhy. Fig. 1 and Riff A (both 4 times)

* Gtr. II doubled by Gtr. IV (elec. w/dist. tone) till Coda.

words— creep up in - side,— creep in - to your mind,— yeah.—

w/Fill 1

So much to say, so much— to say, so much to say, so much— to say.—

w/Fill 1   *D.S. al Coda*

So much to say, so much— to say, so much to say, so much— to say.—   'Cause

w/Rhy. Fig. 1 (4 times)
Coda   w/Riff A (Gtr. II: 4 times; Gtr. IV: 2 times)

w/Fill 1

So much to say, so much— to say, so much to say, so much— to say.—

So much to say, so much— to say, so much to

w/Fill 1

say, so much— to say.—

w/Fill 1

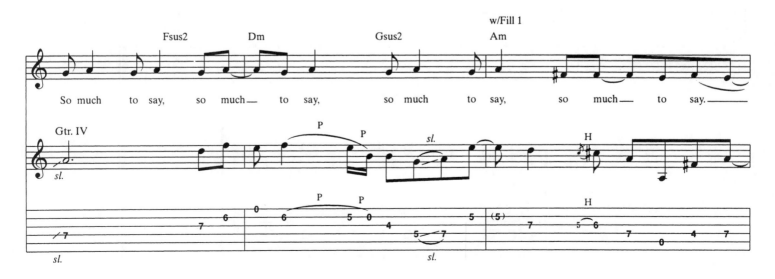

So much to say, so much— to say, so much to say, so much— to say.—

157

SO RIGHT

Words and Music by
David J. Matthews and Glen Ballard

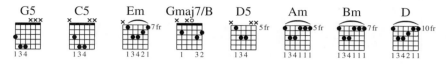

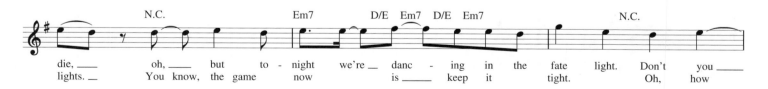

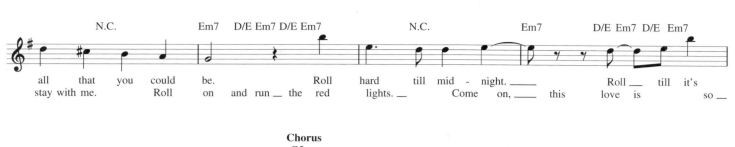

all that you could be. Roll hard till mid - night.___ Roll __ till it's
stay with me. Roll on and run _ the red lights. _ Come on, this love is so _

Chorus
G5
Rhy. Fig. 2

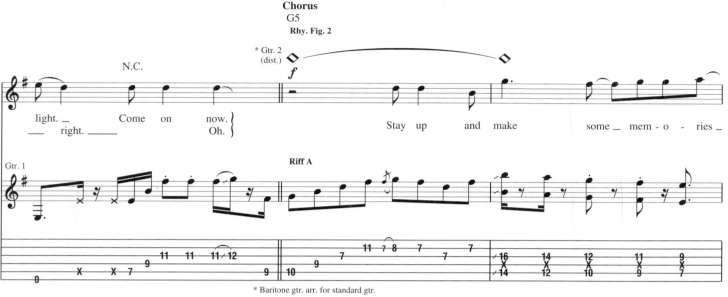

light. _ Come on now. Stay up and make some _ mem - o - ries _
_ right. __ Oh.

Gtr. 1
Riff A

* Baritone gtr. arr. for standard gtr.

C5
Em

_____ here _____ with us _____ now. _____ To roll the

Gmaj7/B
C5
D5
End Rhy. Fig. 2

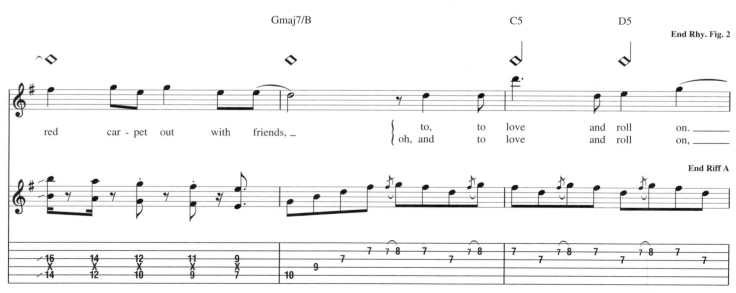

red car - pet out with friends, _ to, to love and roll on. ____
oh, and to love and roll on, _____

End Riff A

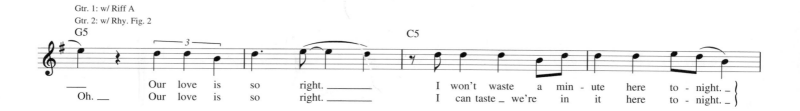

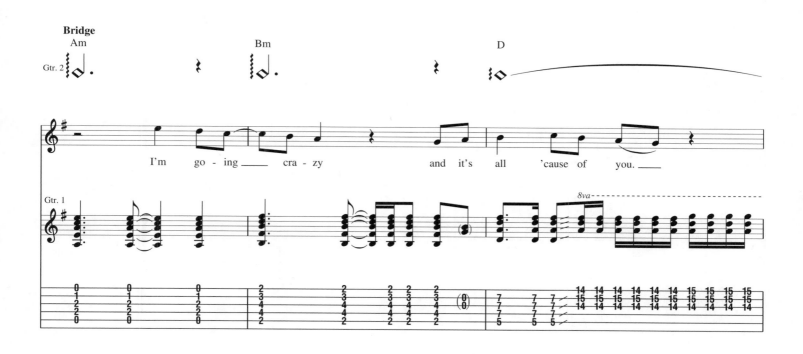

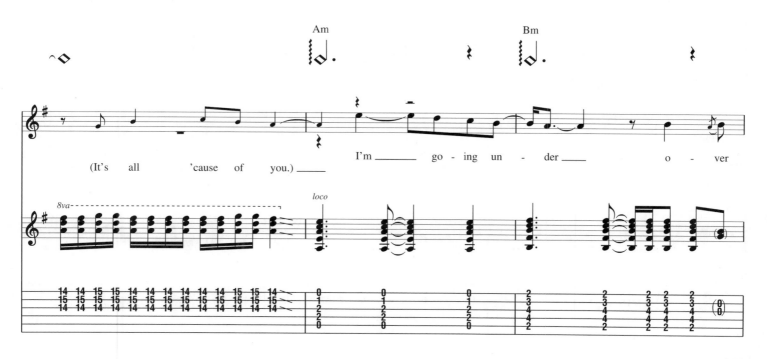

161

live, _____ ev - 'ry - bod - y's trance _____ danc - ing to - night. Oh, _____ so

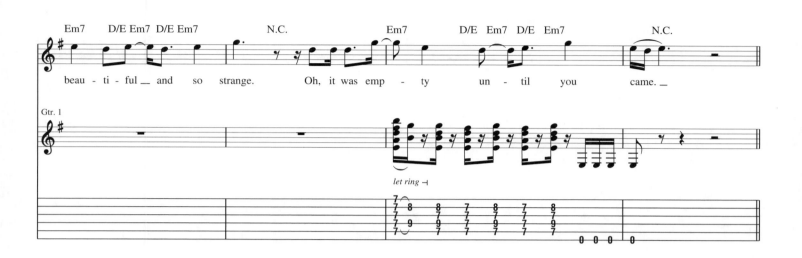

beau - ti - ful _____ and so strange. Oh, it was emp - ty un - til you came. _____

let ring

Chorus

Gtr. 1: w/ Riff A (3 times)
Gtr. 2: w/ Rhy. Fig. 2 (3 times)

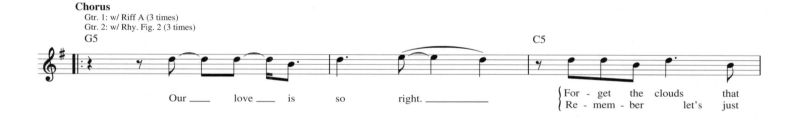

Our _____ love _____ is so right. _____

For - get the clouds that
Re - mem - ber let's just

rain on _____ your _____ light. _____
move to - geth - er.

Our love is so right. _____

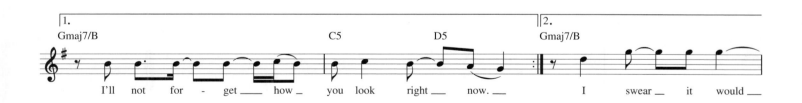

I'll not for - get _____ how _____ you look right _____ now. _____

I swear _____ it would _____

_____ last for - ev - er. _____ Our love is so right. _____

Oh, ___ for-get the clouds that rain down ___ on you. ___ Our love is

so right. ___ Don't ___ be - lieve, don't be - lieve ___ the rain, ___ oh. ___

Outro-Sax Solo

Gtr. 1: w/ Riff A
Gtr. 2: w/ Rhy. Fig. 2

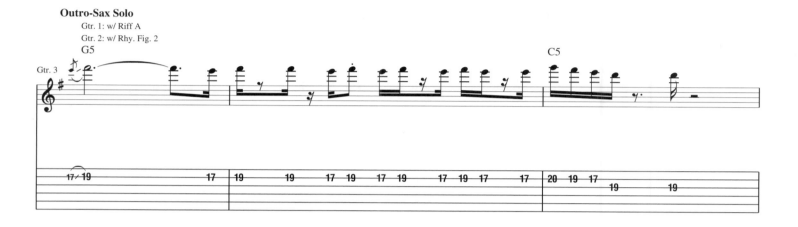

Begin fade

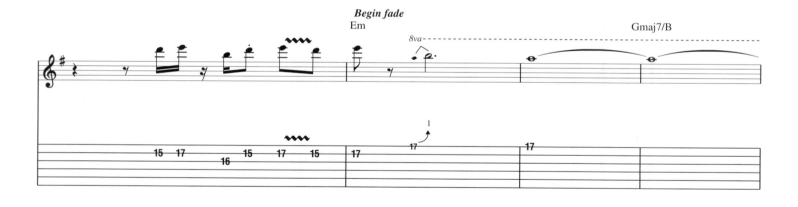

Fade out

Gtr. 1: w/ Riff A (1st 2 meas.)
Gtr. 2: w/ Rhy. Fig. 2 (1st 2 meas.)

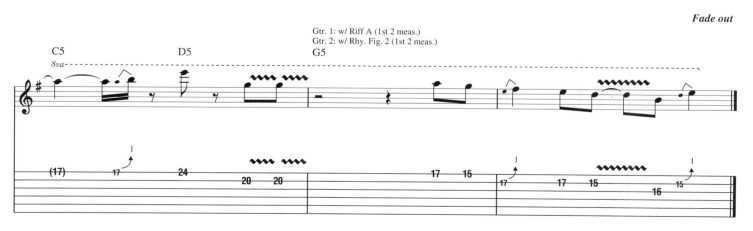

THE SPACE BETWEEN

Words and Music by
David J. Matthews and Glen Ballard

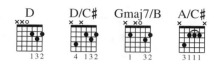

* Baritone gtr. arr. for standard gtr.; doubled throughout (music sounds a 4th lower than indicated).

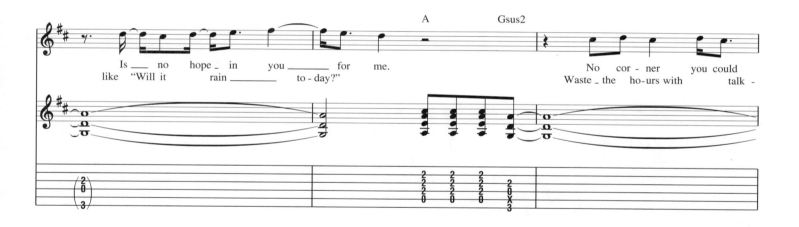

Bridge

Look at us spin-ning out in the mad - ness of a roll - er coast - er. __ You know you went off like the dev - il in a

Fill 1

End Fill 1

* Gtr. 4

Gtr. 1

* Sax arr. for gtr.

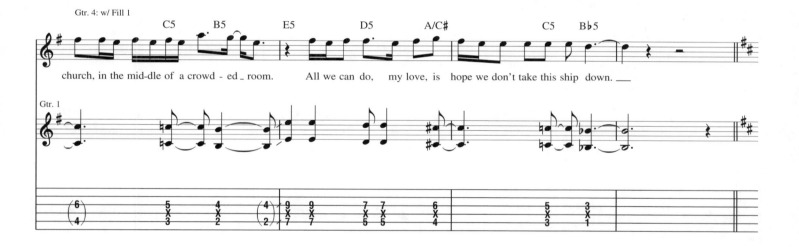

Gtr. 4: w/ Fill 1

church, in the mid-dle of a crowd - ed __ room. All we can do, my love, is hope we don't take this ship down. __

Gtr. 1

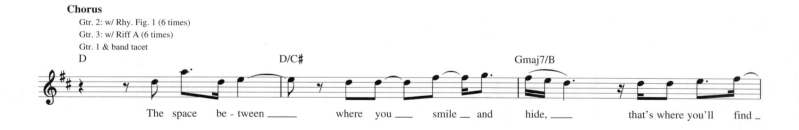

Chorus

Gtr. 2: w/ Rhy. Fig. 1 (6 times)
Gtr. 3: w/ Riff A (6 times)
Gtr. 1 & band tacet

D   D/C#   Gmaj7/B

The space be - tween _____ where you __ smile __ and hide, _____ that's where you'll find _

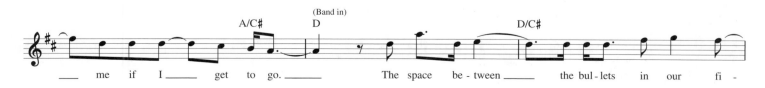

(Band in)

A/C#   D   D/C#

_ me if I ____ get to go. ___ The space be - tween _____ the bul - lets in our fi -

-re fight _____ is where I'll be hid - ing, wait - ing for you. ____ The rain that falls ____

____ splashed _ in your heart, _____ ran ____ like sad - ness _ down the win - dow in - to your

room. The space be - tween ____ our _ wick - ed _ lies ____ is _ where we hope _ to keep safe _ from pain. _

____ Take my _ hand ____ 'cause _ we're walk - ing _____ out ____ of _____ here. ____ Oh,

oh. _____ Right out _ of here, ____ love, ____ is all _____ we need, ____ dear.

Outro-Chorus
Gtr. 2: w/ Rhy. Fig. 1 (2 times)
Gtr. 3: w/ Riff A (2 times)
Band tacet

The space be - tween _____ what's _ wrong and right _____ is where _ you'll find _

____ me hid - ing, wait - ing for you. ____ The space be - tween _____ your _ heart and _

* Gtr. 5

* Bass arr. for gtr.

Repeat and fade

Gtr. 2: w/ Rhy. Fig. 1
Gtr. 3: w/ Riff A
Gtr. 5: w/ Riff B (4 times)

Gtr. 5: w/ Riff B (2 times)

____ mind ____ is the space _ we'll fill with time. The space be - tween. _

STAY (WASTING TIME)

Words and Music by David J. Matthews,
Stefan Lessard and Leroi Moore

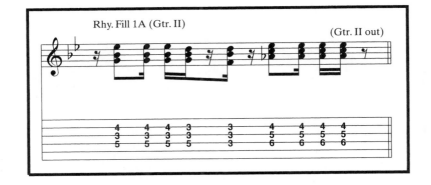

Additional Lyrics

2. Well, then later on the sun began to fade.
   And then, well, the clouds rolled over our heads,
   And it began to rain.
   Oh, we were dancin', mouths open,
   We were splashin' in the tongue taste.
   And for a moment, this good time would never end.
   You and me, you and me...

2nd Chorus:
Just wastin' time.
I was kissin' you, you were kissin' me, love,
From a good day into the moonlight.
Now a night so fine makes us wanna
Stay, stay, stay, stay, stay for a while. *(To Interlude I)*

TOO MUCH

Words by David J. Matthews
Music by David J. Matthews, Carter Beauford,
Stefan Lessard, Leroi Moore and Boyd Tinsley

*Play all repeats and recalled guitar figures w/variations ad lib (throughout)

**Gtr. II to left of slashes.

***Gtr. II is violin arr. for gtr.; Gtr. III is horns arr. for gtr.; Gtr. IV is two gtrs. arr. for one.

*Accented notes are played 1st
time only; omit when recalled.

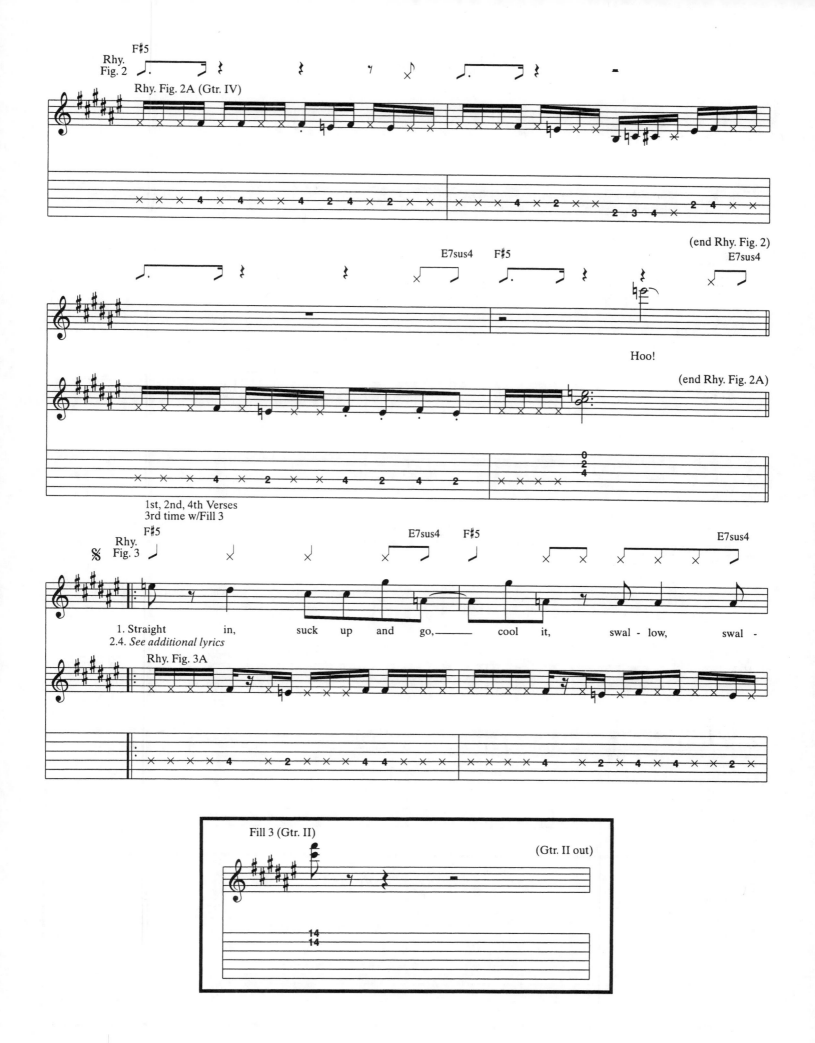

for me, play more, ten times in the same day. I need more.

I'm going over my borders. Gonna take more, more from you, letter by letter.

(cont. in slashes)

184

Suck it up, suck it up.—

Gtr. II

Gtr. III

Gtr. IV substitute Rhy. Fill 4

Suck it up, suck it up, suck it up, yeah.

(Gtr. II out)

Suck it up,— suck it up, suck it up.

Gtr. III

Suck it up, suck it up, suck it up, suck it up, ba - by.

Additional Lyrics

2. Oh, traffic jam, got more cars than a beach got sand.
   Suck it up, suck it up, suck it up,
   Fill it up until no more.
   I'm no crazy creep.
   I've got it coming to me because I'm not satisfied.
   The hunger keeps on growing. *(To Chorus)*

4. I told God, "I'm coming to your country.
   I'm going to eat up your cities,
   Your homes, you know."
   I've got a stomach full,
   It's not a chip on my shoulder.
   I've got this growl in my tummy
   And I'm gonna stop it today. *(To Chorus)*

TRIPPING BILLIES

Words and Music by
David J. Matthews

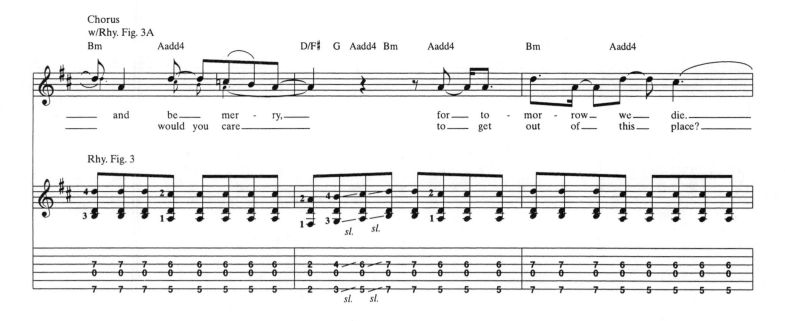

Chorus
w/Rhy. Fig. 3A

— and be mer-ry, for to-mor-row we die.
would you care to get out of this place?

Rhy. Fig. 3

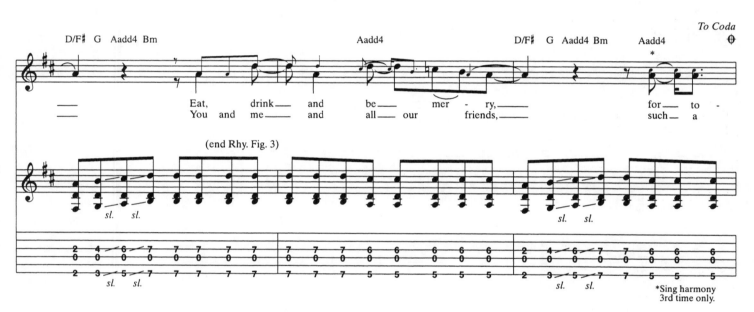

To Coda ⊕

— Eat, drink and be mer-ry, for to-
— You and me and all our friends, such a

(end Rhy. Fig. 3)

*Sing harmony
3rd time only.

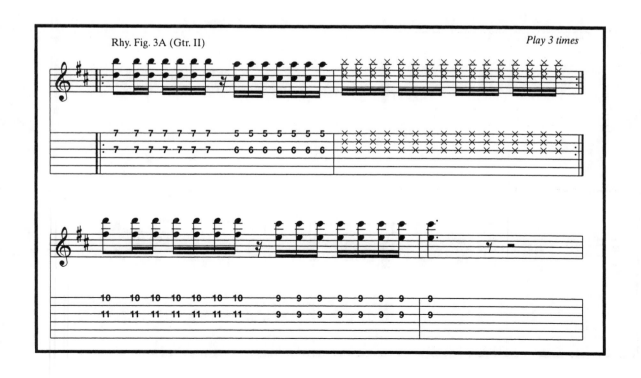

Rhy. Fig. 3A (Gtr. II)   Play 3 times

192

193

Additional Lyrics

2. We're wearing nothing,
   Nothing but our shadows.
   Shadows falling down on the beach sand.
   Remembering once,
   Out on the beaches,
   We wore pineapple grass bracelets. *(To Chorus)*

3. We are all sitting,
   Legs crossed 'round a fire.
   My yellow flame, she dances.
   Tequila drinking,
   Oh, our minds will wander
   To wondrous places. *(To Chorus)*

194

TWO STEP

Words and Music by
David J. Matthews

Moderately ♩ = 120

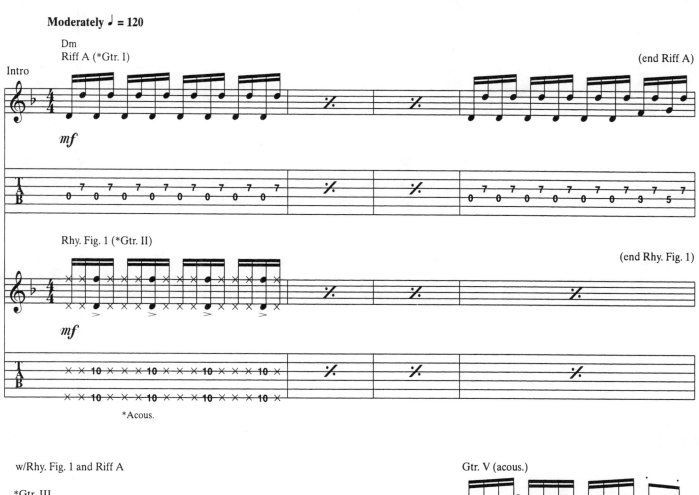

*Acous.

*Gtrs. III & IV are acous. w/drop-D tuning: ⑥ = D.

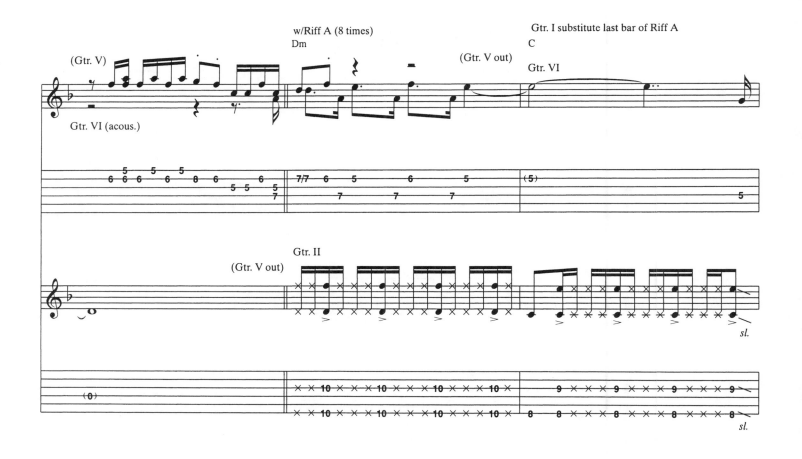

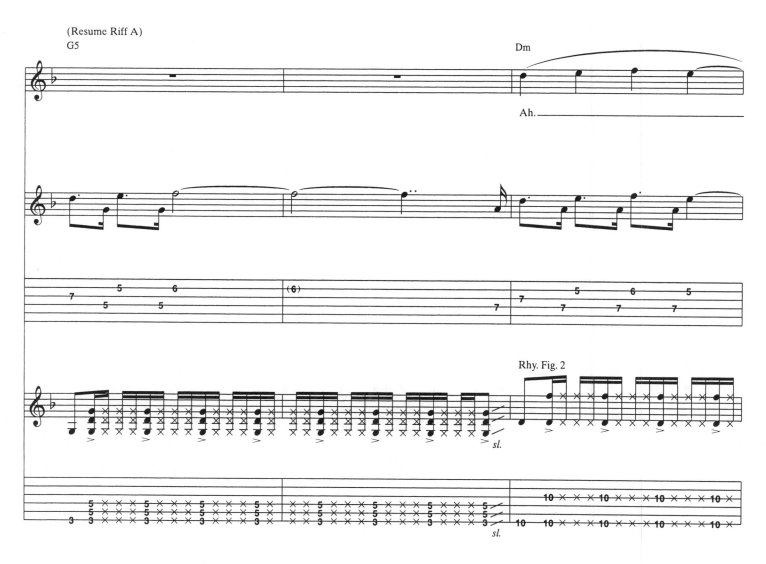

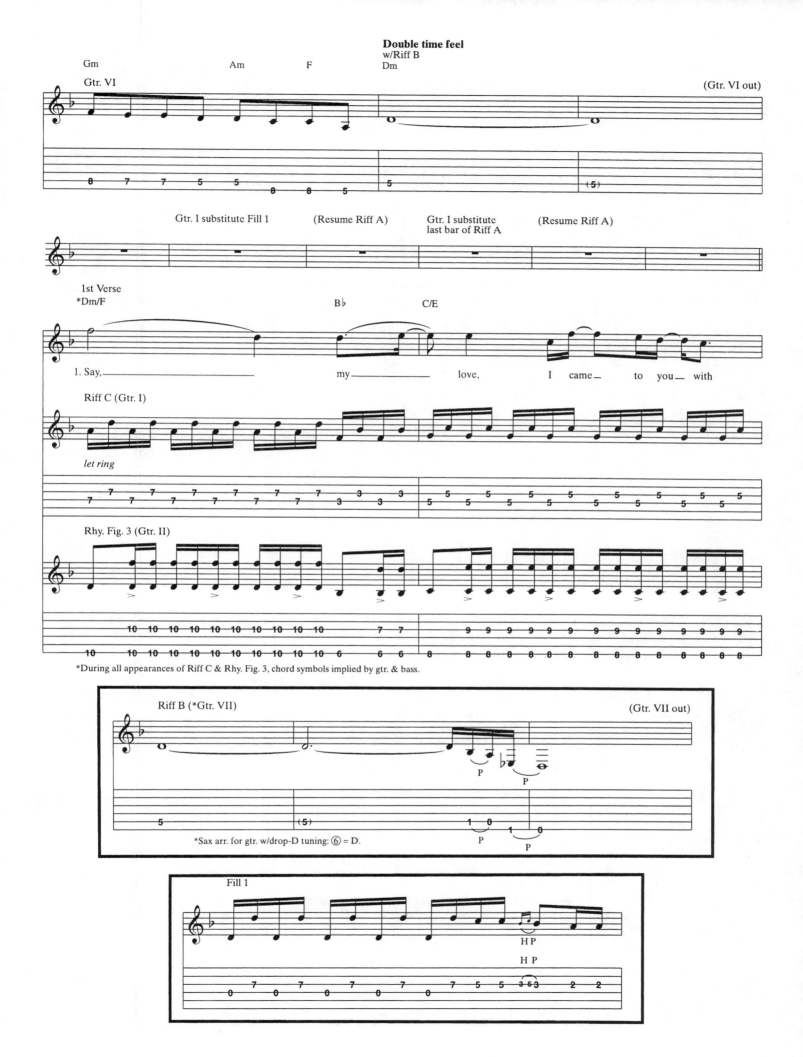

202

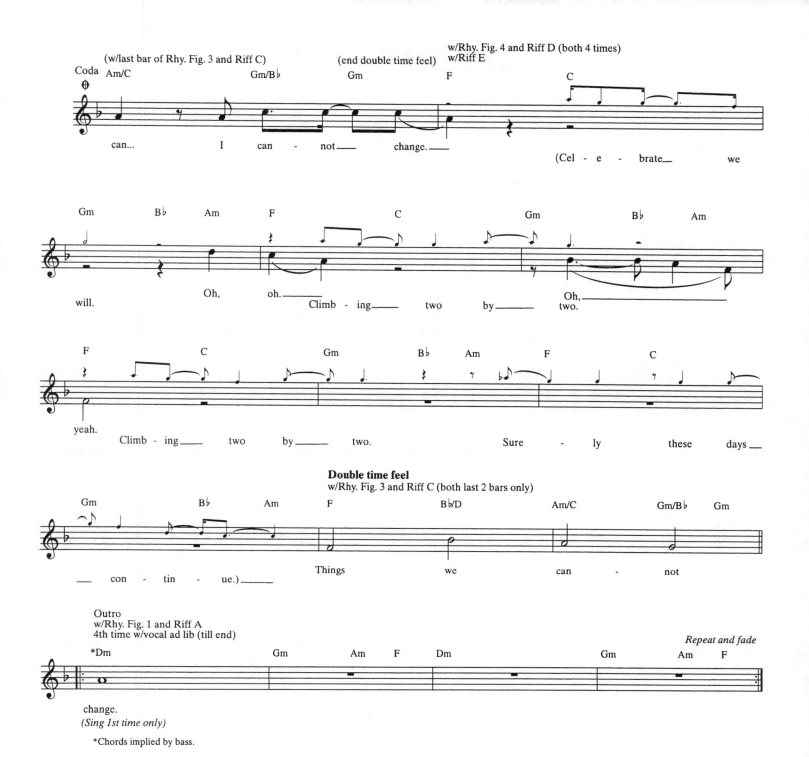

Additional Lyrics

3. Hey, my love, you came to me like
   Wine comes to this mouth,
   Grown tired of water all the time.
   You quench my heart and, oh, you
   Quench my mind. *(To Chorus)*

4. Oh, my love, I came to you
   With best intentions.
   You lay down and give to me
   Just what I'm seeking.
   Say, love, watch me celebrate. *(To Chorus)*

WAREHOUSE

Words and Music by
David J. Matthews

209

Additional Lyrics

3. Hey, we have found
   Becoming one in a million.
   Slip into the crowd.
   This question I found in the gap in the sidewalk.

   2nd Pre-chorus:
   Keep all your sights on.
   Hey, the black cat changing colors.
   And you can walk under ladders.
   And swim as the tide choose to turn you. *(To Chorus)*

4. Shut up, I'm thinking.
   I had a clue, now it's gone forever.
   Sitting over these bones,
   You can read in whatever. You're needing to...

   3rd Pre-chorus:
   Keep all your sights on.
   Yeah, man, the black cat changing colors.
   When it's not the colours that matter,
   but that they'll all fade away.

   2rd Chorus:
   And I, life goes on.
   End of tunnel, TV set, spot in the middle.
   Static fade, statistical bit.
   Soon I'll fade away, I'll fade away.
   Oh, but this I admit.
   Seems so good, hard to believe an end to it.
   The warehouse is bare, nothing, it's all inside of it.
   The walls and halls have disappeared, they've disappeared. Well.
   My love, I'd love to stay here, *etc.*

WHAT WOULD YOU SAY

Words and Music by
David J. Matthews

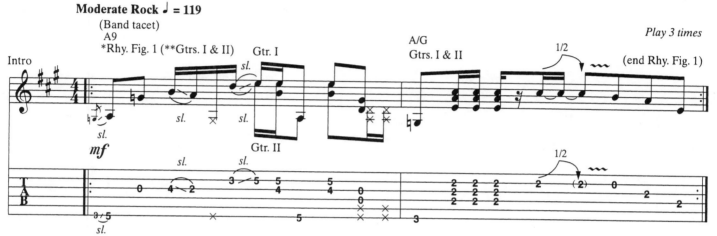

*When recalled, Rhy. Fig. 1 includes slight variations ad lib.
**Gtrs. I & II are acoustic.

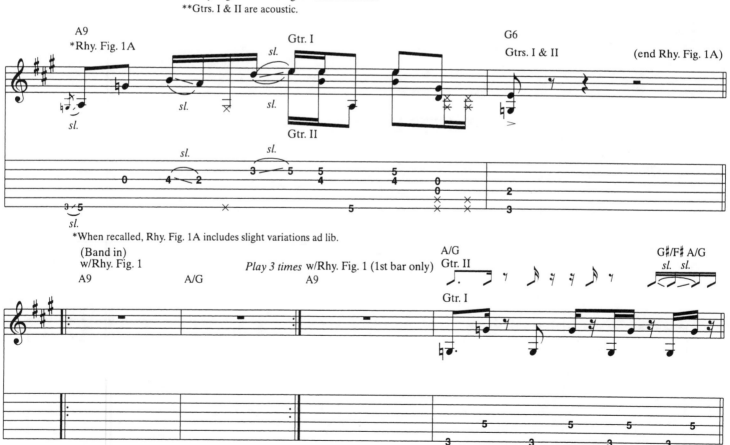

*When recalled, Rhy. Fig. 1A includes slight variations ad lib.

1st, 2nd, 3rd Verses
w/Rhy. Fig. 1 (3½ times)
3rd time w/Fill 1

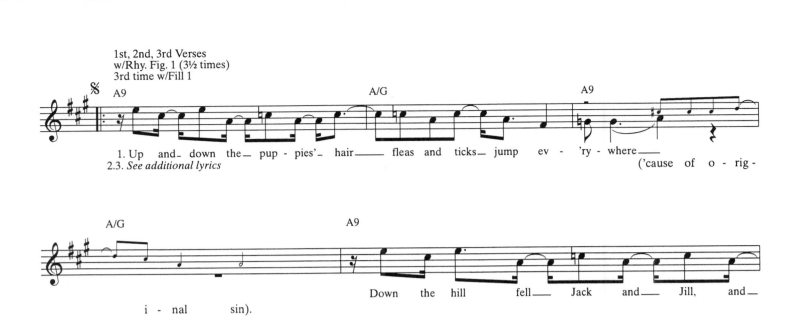

1. Up and down the pup - pies' hair___ fleas and ticks___ jump ev - 'ry - where___ ('cause of o - rig -
2.3. *See additional lyrics*

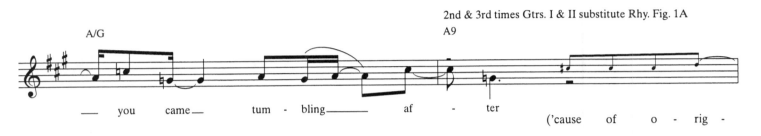

Down the hill fell___ Jack and___ Jill, and___

i - nal sin).

2nd & 3rd times Gtrs. I & II substitute Rhy. Fig. 1A

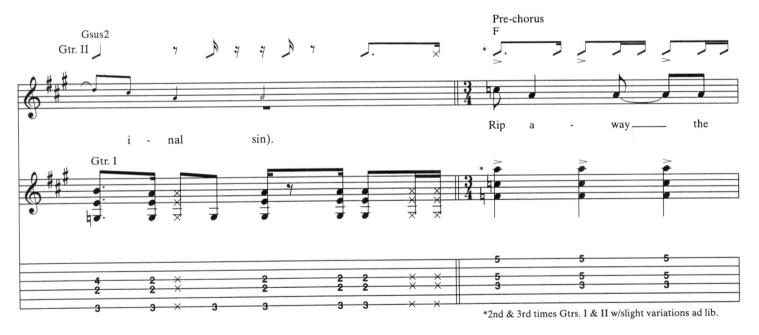

___ you came___ tum - bling___ af - ter ('cause of o - rig -

Pre-chorus

i - nal sin).

Rip a - way___ the

*2nd & 3rd times Gtrs. I & II w/slight variations ad lib.

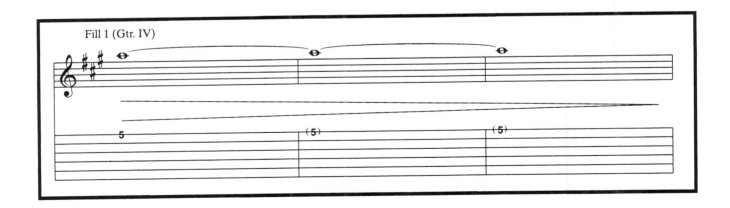

Fill 1 (Gtr. IV)

Chorus
w/Rhy. Fig. 2
2nd time Gtrs. I & II substitute Rhy. Fig. 1

Don't drop the big___ one.
If you a mon-key on a

Rhy. Fig. 1B (Gtrs. I & II)   Gtr. I
Gtr. II

(end Rhy. Fig. 1B)

*Gtr. I to left of slashes in TAB.

**When Rhy. Fig. 1B is recalled,
substitute muted strings for
chords in parentheses.

1st time w/Rhy. Fig. 1B (2 times)
2nd time w/Rhy. Fig. 1 (2 times)

well, don't cut my life - line.
string,   If you a dog-gie on a chain,

well, don't bite the mail -
w/Rhy. Fig. 1   1st time Gtr. I substitute Rhy. Fill 2

man.___   What___ would you say?___

Rhy. Fig. 2 (Gtr. III)

Rhy. Fill 2 (Gtr. I)

216

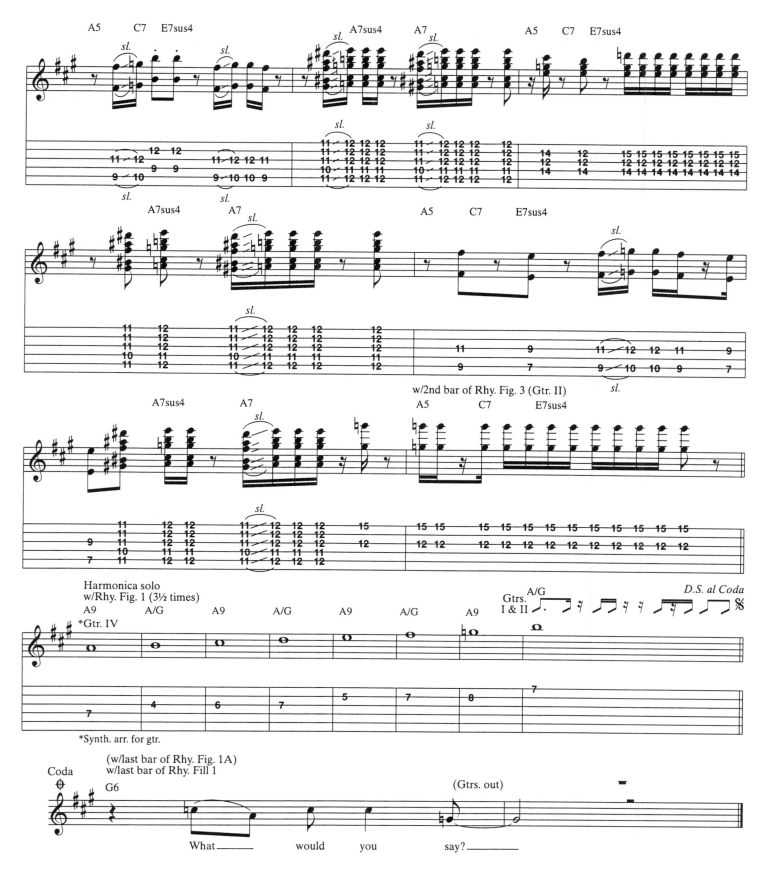

Additional Lyrics

2.3. I was there when the bear ate his head, thought it was a candy.
(Everyone goes in the end.)
Knock, knock on the door. Who's it for? There's nobody in here.
(Look in the mirror, my friend.)

2nd, 3rd Pre-chorus:
I don't understand, at best, and cannot speak for all the rest.
The morning rise, a lifetime's passed me by.
 What would you say?

WHERE ARE YOU GOING

Lyrics by David J. Matthews
Music by Dave Matthews Band

Intro
Moderately slow ♩ = 100

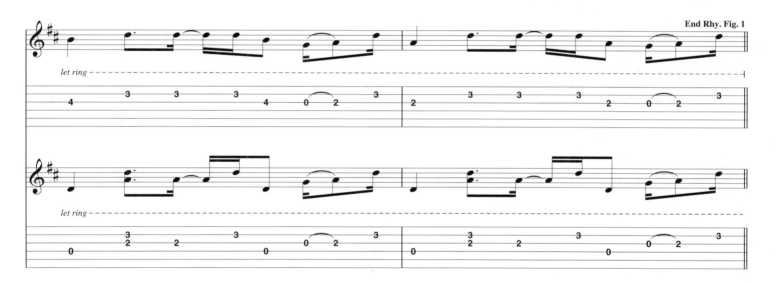

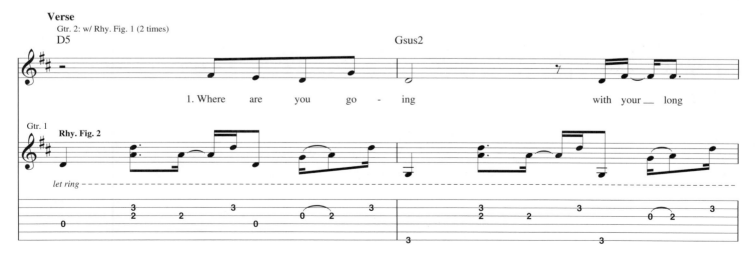

221